LIVERPOOL
A BACKPASS THROUGH THE 1980S

sona BOOKS

© Danann Media Publishing Ltd 2021

First Published by Danann Media Publishing Limited 2014.
© Design Danann media publishing ltd 2021

WARNING: For private domestic use only, any unauthorised Copying, hiring, lending or public performance of this book set is illegal.

CAT NO: SON0518

Photography courtesy of
The Press Association,
Getty Images
Bob Thomas/Getty Images
Popperfoto/Getty Images
Paul Popper/Popperfoto
Allsport UK /Allsport
Ben Radford/Allsport
Photoshot

Certain material © ITV Sport
Book layout & design Darren Grice at Ctrl-d

All rights reserved. No Part of this title may be reproduced or transmitted in any material form (including photocopying or storing it in any medium by electronic means and whether or not transiently or incidentally to some other use of this publication) without the written permission of the copyright owner, except in accordance with the provisions of the Copyright, Designs and Patents Act 1988. Applications for the copyright owner's written permission should be addressed to the publisher.

Made in EU.
978-1-912918-81-2

CONTENTS

- 8   **INTRODUCTION:** LIVERPOOL'S DECADE OF HIGHLIGHTS
- 10   **JUST WARMING UP:** 1979/80
- 22   **SNAKES AND LADDERS:** 1980/81
- 34   **BACK TO THE TOP:** 1981/82
- 44   **THE END OF THE PAISLEY ERA:** 1982/83
- 54   **GOOD THINGS COME IN THREES:** 1983/84
- 66   **THE ONE THAT GOT AWAY:** 1984/85
- 76   **ROSES ARE RED, THE FA CUP IS, TOO!** 1985/86
- 84   **IF YOU HAVE TEARS…:** 1986/87
- 94   **MASTERS OF THE LEAGUE:** 1987/88
- 104   **THE BLUES SEE RED:** 1988/89
- 114   **ONE MORE FOR THE ROAD:** 1989/90
- 124   **EPILOGUE & A FEW MORE STATS:**

INTRODUCTION:
LIVERPOOL'S DECADE OF HIGHLIGHTS

Isn't it just wonderful to sit back and revel in those magical times from the past, without worrying about what has gone before or what is still to come? No one to interrupt you as you innocently while away some happy moments remembering the good things in life? Well, this book is meant to help you do just that. Unashamedly nostalgic, unashamedly upbeat, unashamedly red, this book is an all - too-brief reminder of what happened once upon time at a special place in Liverpool that is known as Anfield ….

The colour of football in the 1980s was without doubt red. Liverpool swept up trophies at an astonishing rate as players of world-class quality displayed their skills for the Anfield faithful; Kenny Dalglish, Ian Rush, John Barnes, Alan Hansen, Graeme Souness to mention but a few. They powered the Liverpool teams as the club became the most successful in the history of the game.

The statistics of the decade tell the story and they are astounding:

Between 1980 and 1990 Liverpool won 16 major trophies; they won the League Championship seven times and lifted the League Cup for a record four consecutive seasons; they won the FA Cup in 1986 and 1989; they were champions of Europe twice; they won the Football League Super Cup; they won the Charity Shield five times. In 1983/84 they won the League, the League Cup and the European Cup, and in 1985/86 they won the League and FA Cup double.

They conceded just 24 goals in the 1987/88 season, the third lowest statistic in their history. (1893/94: 18 against: 1968/69: 24 against: 1970/71: 24 against: 1978/79: 16 against). In the same season they won the most points ever; 90, and lost just 2 league games (Everton and Nottingham Forest). Ian Rush scored 47 goals in the 1983/84 season, the most ever scored by a Liverpool player.

Guided – and often yelled at, on and off the pitch – by three managers of outstanding ability, Bob Paisley, Joe Fagan and Kenny Dalglish, and roared on by the Kop, the Liverpool squads of the 80s delivered moments, matches and whole seasons of pure football genius over this period of almost constant success. Every fan will have a favourite goal, player and game, but some events will remain indisputably the best, indelibly written into the history of the club. So, here's a summary in mini format as representative of that classic Liverpool era.

Who can ever forget that night when Real Madrid were vanquished in the European Champions Cup in 1981 after Bayern Munich had also fallen to the Red wave in the semi-final? Unforgettable, too, the 81/82 season, when the magnificent Ian Rush became top goalscorer for the first time with 30 goals and Everton were beaten twice in the League 3-1.

And what about the first ever Wembley clash between Liverpool and Everton in the 1984 League Cup final? That will always be remembered with joy. So will the two Liverpool victories in FA Cup finals; the first in 1986 – and no one will forget the teamwork for which Liverpool were renowned that led to the superb goal by Ian Rush in that cup final – and 1989. Fate is a wonderful thing, sometimes, because they were both against Everton.

What could beat the astonishing 1983/84 season with the League Championship won for the third successive season, the League Cup and the Graeme Souness goal that beat Everton, plus the nerve-shredding European Cup won on penalties to cheer about?

Or perhaps your favourites are in that wonderful season of 1985/86 when Everton were beaten 3-1, Liverpool leaving it until the 57th minute for Rush to score an equaliser in the FA Cup final that gave Liverpool the double?

Poor Fulham in September 1986, you certainly haven't forgotten that? 10-1. And 6 undefeated games against Everton; two in the league, twice in the English Super Cup (7-2 to Liverpool on aggregate) and once in the Charity Shield and League Cup.

In 1988, Peter Beardsley mesmerised fans with his goal in the incredible 5-0 dissection of Nottingham Forest, and a there was a John Barnes performance that took the fans' breath away. Liverpool teamwork fed by individual brilliance was never more in evidence than when Arsenal were beaten 2-0 at Anfield in January 1988. The build up to the first goal by Aldridge was magical.

In 1989 every single match in the FA Cup run was won, and the challenge ended with another victory against Everton in a tense final that went into extra time until Ian Rush came to the rescue with another tour de force and two goals after Aldridge had scored just 4 minutes into the game. What a treat to see those two in action!

And in 1990 the Reds delivered a 9-goal feast against Crystal Palace; 8 Liverpool players scored, with Steve Nicol topping and tailing the fun with his two.

But it seemed that there was a price to pay for this largesse from the football gods over the decade. Liverpool fans were present in two of football's worst tragedies; one at the Heysel Stadium in 1985 in the European Cup Final between Liverpool and Juventus when 39 people died and 600 were injured, and then at Hillsborough in 1989 when 96 people died and 766 were injured.

Liverpool were a magical side to watch in the 80s. It was such an extraordinary and exciting decade for Liverpool FC that it is tempting to dive into the goody bag right at the start and bathe freely in the greatest nostalgic highlights. There are so many of them after all. But we shall resist, be patient, and start where it is right and proper to start, at the beginning, so that the real highlights when they come are given their proper perspective.

Which means that we have to look at the very first matches of the 1979/80 season … painful, yes, but just think of the rewards!

JUST WARMING UP:
THE 1979/80 SEASON

It is the 21st of August 1979. Liverpool launch their league challenge on the back of four league titles during the seventies. They had won the Championship the previous season, having been on the number one spot since the second game, and they had just beaten Arsenal in the English Charity Shield, on the 11th of August, so there was already some serious winning going on. Bob Paisley was in his fifth year in charge and had three League Championships, one FA Cup, two European Cups, a UEFA Cup and a European Super Cup under his belt.

Expectations were high.

Bolton Wanderers held the Reds to a 0-0 draw. At Anfield. A dampener if ever there was one. Still, West Brom went down 3-1, also at Anfield, four days later. Better. And then … a loss, 3-1 to Southampton, who finished the season in 14th place. Come on lads, pull your socks up!

This stumbling start continued through to September when Nottingham Forest beat Liverpool 1-0 and dumped them onto 9th place. It really was not looking at all good for the league champions. Their form in the League Cup competition was hardly inspiring either. They needed two bites at Tranmere Rovers before they eventually polished them off 4-0, and despite improved form, the Reds fell to Nottingham Forest in the semi-final in February 1980.

Dinamo Tbilisi put paid to the European Champions Cup, beating Liverpool 2-4 on aggregate in October. After that, the team rallied and began the climb up the league table to the top, which they reached in November, lost for two games and then reclaimed in December with a 3-1 victory over Aston Villa at Villa Park.

The English FA Cup drive was stopped by Arsenal in the semi-final after four matches were needed to decide the winner by a single goal, following two 1-1 draws and one 0-0 game.

Nor was there so much to cheer about in the derby games. The matches were played against an Everton team that narrowly missed relegation on 19th place that season. In October 1979, the Reds could only manage a draw against Everton 2-2 at Anfield. Come March 1980, however, the Reds did the decent thing and came away from Goodison Park with a 2-1 victory. Johnson and Neal were the scorers with Neal scoring from a penalty. Blushes were spared by that.

Despite five more losses before the end of the season, the Reds held that first position throughout and squeaked home with 60 points, two ahead of northern rivals Manchester United; and they were unbeaten at home for the second consecutive year.

The 1st of May 1980 is marked down as a very special month in Liverpool memories; that was when a man who would become one of the great Liverpool legends was signed up. None other than the mighty Ian Rush arrived for a fee of £300,000.

And it was a glorious season for Terry McDermott. On scintillating form, he was voted player of the year by both the press and players. David Johnson was top goalscorer with 27 and Kenny Dalglish, who had been top goalscorer for two consecutive seasons, had 23.

11th August 1979 FA Charity Shield Football. Liverpool v Arsenal

PLAYER DEBUTS

Two players donned red shirts for the first time; on the 25th August 1979, Colin Irwin ran out against West Bromwich Albion, and on the 15th of September 1979, Avi Cohen started against Leeds United. (Avi Cohen was killed in a motorcycle crash in Israel on the 29th December 2010.) 18-year-old Ronnie Whelan arrived on the 19th September 1979 but would not make his debut until April 3rd 1981.

1980. Avi Cohen

Top rivals in the league this season were Manchester United, Ipswich Town, Arsenal and Nottingham Forest,

and the final table looked like this:

POS	TEAM	POINTS	GD
1	Liverpool	60	+51
2	Man. United	58	+30
3	Ipswich Town	53	+29
4	Arsenal	52	+16
5	Nott. Forest	48	+20

The final team in the top five for Liverpool to have a crack at was Nottingham Forest, and the initial attempt came on the 29th of September 1979. As a forecast of the future it was a bad omen. Liverpool went to Forest hoping to get some traction on the season only to go down 1-0.

Next up were Ipswich Town on away turf, and this time Liverpool came home with a 2-1 win.

Following a 2-2 draw at Anfield against Everton, in which Terry McDermott and Gary Stanley had the honour of being the first players to be sent off in a twentieth century derby, and then a 0-0 draw against Arsenal, Liverpool's fight back had well and truly begun, and they were swiftly climbing the table. By the time they met Manchester United in December at Anfield, they had already taken over the top spot and cemented it with a 2-0 win.

Nottingham Forest popped up again at Anfield in February 1980 and were sent home with a 2-0 defeat to savour thanks to McDermott, who scored in the 80th minute, and a Ray Kennedy goal in the 84th. That was followed four days later by a sobering 1-1 draw at home to Ipswich. Manchester United made the season uncomfortable with a 2-1 win at Old Trafford in April 1980 and when Arsenal could only be held to a 1-1 draw at Anfield, it meant that Liverpool and United were going to be neck and neck on the final straight. (Another draw at Crystal Palace held the tension until a 4-1 walloping of Aston Villa put the Reds beyond reach and they could afford to lose the final game 1-0 against Middlesborough.)

11th August 1979 - Charity Shield - Liverpool v Arsenal - Alan Kennedy on the ball

THE STATISTICAL SEASON:

NUMBER OF GAMES:
Played	60
Won	35
Drawn	15
Lost	10

CLEAN SHEETS:
League	19
All Matches	27

GOALS SCORED:
League	81
All Matches	111

AVERAGE NUMBER OF GOALS SCORED IN EACH MATCH:
League	2.19
All Matches	2.32

AVERAGE NUMBER OF MINUTES REQUIRED FOR GOALS SCORED:
League	48
All Matches	50

AVERAGE HOME ATTENDANCE:
League	44,578
All Matches	42,233

CLASSIC MATCHES: 1979/80

LIVERPOOL V ARSENAL 3-1:
Charity Shield: Wembley, 11th August 1979

This was to be the first clash between Liverpool and Arsenal in the FA Charity Shield. It was a day when Liverpool outclassed their London rivals and proved why they were one of the best teams in England at the time. At times, their domination was absolute, with Terry McDermott, David Johnson and Kenny Dalglish in sparkling form.

Arsenal's dangerman Liam Brady couldn't make an impact, because Souness was on his every move and in control in midfield, and Ray Kennedy was an ever-present threat on the wing.

McDermott got the Reds on the score sheet in the 38th minute when he picked up a pass from Ray Kennedy and took the ball to within 25 yards of the goal from where he struck a low, fierce drive that Pat Jennings in the Arsenal goal could do nothing to stop.

When the second half started, fans had to wait until the 63rd minute for Alan Hansen to charge up the field as far as the Arsenal penalty area, where Kenny Dalglish was waiting to beat an Arsenal defender and put home the second goal.

Just two minutes later, Liverpool surged again with first Dalglish and then Johnson helping to give McDermott his second goal.

A consolation goal was netted by Alan Sunderland for the Gunners.

1 **Ray Clemence** Goalkeeper
2 **Phil Neal** Defender
3 **Alan Kennedy** Defender
4 **Phil Thompson** Defender
5 **Ray Kennedy** Midfielder/Forward
6 **Alan Hansen** Defender
7 **Kenny Dalglish** Forward
8 **Jimmy Case** Forward
9 **David Johnson** Forward
10 **Terry McDermott** Midfielder
11 **Graeme Souness** Midfielder
16 **Steve Ogrizovic** Goalkeeper
14 **Avi Cohen** Defender
12 **Steve Heighway** Winger
13 **Sammy Lee** Midfielder
15 **David Fairclough** Forward

LIVERPOOL V CRYSTAL PALACE 3-0:
League Division One: Anfield, 15th December 1979

With Palace only just back in the First Division they were off to a cracking start and were third in the league when they met up with Liverpool. They had a tough fight on their hands. The Reds piled on the pressure, and Johnson, Dalglish and teammates came dangerously close on many occasions with their exciting, flowing football. Jimmy Case fired a mighty free kick that threatened to take Palace keeper Burridge with it as he saved Palace with a terrific save early on. Brave Burridge he might have been called as he threw himself fearlessly across his goal to prevent a flurry of Liverpool attacks from ending in success.

Then, as the first half ebbed away, Liverpool pressure became intense. The ball came to Johnson on the outside and he sent over a pinpoint cross to the head of Case, whose long accurate header finally left the Palace keeper with no chance.

The second goal went in early in the second half after hard work by Dalglish had won him a corner. Case put over a ball that caused all manner of confusion around the Palace box. Hansen headed the ball back into the danger zone, and it was Dalglish the unstoppable, who again fought a lone battle, besieged by Palace players, before he worked his magic and sent a chipped ball towards and into the net. It was a classic beauty to watch, the work of a razor-edged striker.

Beautiful to behold, also, was the wonderful fast passing move by Liverpool that ripped open the Palace defence, and McDermott came hurtling in only to see his shot thwarted by Burridge's legs.

11th August 1979. Graeme Souness, Alan Hansen and Kenny Dalglish with the Charity Shield

But not even Burridge could prevent another Liverpool surge and a precision pass between midfielder Souness and Ray Kennedy ending in two Liverpool forwards, McDermott and Johnson, clear and ready to strike side by side. McDermott got to the ball first and that was Liverpool's third.

Burridge had to work equally as hard thereafter or there would have been more goals still.

1 Ray Clemence Goalkeeper
2 Phil Neal Defender
3 Alan Kennedy Defender
4 Phil Thompson Midfielder
5 Ray Kennedy Midfielder
6 Alan Hansen Defender
7 Kenny Dalglish Forward
8 Jimmy Case Forward
9 David Johnson Forward
10 Terry McDermott Midfielder
11 Graeme Souness Midfielder
12 Steve Heighway Winger

LIVERPOOL V MANCHESTER UNITED 2-0:

League Division One: Anfield, 26th December 1979

Alan Hansen and David Johnson were the heroes of this great victory against northern rivals Manchester United. Hansen considered his goal in the fifteenth minute to be the best of his career up until then. He scored 14 for Liverpool in his career with the red shirt. The man who gave Bob Paisley more heart attacks than anyone else, moved forward in his inimitable long-legged style to take a return ball from Ray Kennedy and score the first for the Reds.

United almost equalised when Gary Bailey belted a goal kick that bounced over Clemence's head. Luckily the keeper was spared more than a red face when the ball hit the crossbar and went over. It was Bailey who was then left red-faced when he mishandled a David Johnson attempt at goal five minutes from time and allowed the ball to wiggle into the net.

It was Liverpool's 47th home win against United.

1 Ray Clemence Goalkeeper
2 Phil Neal Defender
3 Alan Kennedy Defender
4 Phil Thompson Midfielder
5 Ray Kennedy Midfielder
6 Alan Hansen Defender
7 Kenny Dalglish Forward
8 Jimmy Case Forward
9 David Johnson Forward
10 Terry McDermott Midfielder

NORWICH CITY V LIVERPOOL 3-5:

League Division One: Carrow Road, 9th February 1980
And what a cracker this match was!

Clemence was beaten before he had even touched the ball as Martin Peters put Norwich ahead after less than two minutes with a header following a corner kick and stunned the Liverpool crowd. They needn't have worried. But they were in for an incredible afternoon.

Barely three minutes passed and Liverpool drew level through David Fairclough, who ran into space on the right hand side of the penalty area and drove home a superb left-foot shot.

Liverpool put on a display of inventive football before setting up the next goal. With just 18 minutes played, Hansen made another of his rare but often lethal runs, into the Norwich penalty area to slide a terrific pass in front of Fairclough, who again struck a beautiful shot into the right-hand corner of the net. (Incidentally, a Hansen blunder in the second half when he practically gave the ball to Norwich in his own half almost let the men in

3rd May 1980. Liverpool v Aston Villa, Phil Neal plays the ball as Aston Villa looks on

yellow strike again. Swings and roundabouts!)

When Reeves struck with a headed goal for Norwich just after the half hour mark it was the last goal before the half-time whistle.

The fun continued in the second half with Fairclough getting his hat trick after Dalgish had ripped down the left wing into the penalty box and impudently crossed the ball through the Norwich defence straight to the feet of the Liverpool striker.

On 76 minutes, John Fashanu kept the tension high with a scorching, curving volley into the right-hand corner of the Liverpool net, which Clemence hadn't a cat's hope in hell of getting to. 3-3 and the attacks moved like waves from end to end.

To the delight of Liverpool fans, the Norwich joy lasted just over ten minutes. Dalglish popped in the Liverpool fourth with a header from close range that he struck when he was almost kneeling on the ground.

Norwich had no more answers, but Liverpool hadn't finished yet. It was Case, making up for an earlier near miss, who put the result beyond doubt sixty seconds later in the 89th minute. He beat off heavy opposition in the penalty area to whack home the fifth goal and put an end to a wonderful afternoon of football and also Norwich City's unbeaten home record.

1 Ray Clemence Goalkeeper
2 Phil Neal Defender
3 Alan Kennedy Defender
4 Phil Thompson Midfielder
5 Ray Kennedy Defender
6 Alan Hansen Defender
7 Kenny Dalglish Forward
8 Jimmy Case Forward
9 David Fairclough Forward
10 Terry McDermott Midfielder
11 Sammy Lee Midfielder
12 Steve Heighway Winger

LIVERPOOL V ASTON VILLA 4-1:
League Division One: Anfield, 3rd May 1980

This match will live in the memory for two reasons; it secured the Championship for the Reds, and Avi Cohen had the unfortunate honour of scoring for both sides! It was also a repeat scenario from twelve months previously when the Reds had played Villa, needing a win to become champions.

The Reds, who had to win this match to retain the Championship, got off to a lively start and were ahead after three minutes through a David Johnson goal, which, as he said later, he lashed at the goal and "… it hit the post and shot across into the net". Everyone is glad when Lady Luck dons a red shirt now and again!

Avi Cohen made it one all when he scored his debut goal … for the Villains, unfortunately, in the 26th minute. Ouch, you had to feel sorry for him even when you wished him to be banished to another planet. Everyone was glad that he hadn't been, of course, even though they had to wait until the second half before Cohen scored his debut goal at the Kop end for the Reds on the 50th minute. The game was more or less over after another David Johnson goal made it three for Liverpool. The icing on the cake was provided by Villa man Noel Blake, who decided to emulate Cohen and get a goal in his own net to make the final result 4-1. Liverpool were League Champions for the second successive year. It was Paisley's fourth title as Liverpool manager.

I bet Avi dreaded the 26th minute of a match ever after!

1 Ray Clemence Goalkeeper
2 Phil Neal Defender
3 Avi Cohen Defender
4 Phil Thompson Defender
5 Ray Kennedy Midfielder
6 Alan Hansen Defender
7 Kenny Dalglish Forward
8 Sammy Lee Midfielder
9 David Johnson Forward
10 Terry McDermott Midfielder
11 Graeme Souness Midfielder
12 Howard Gayle Forw/Midf/Wing

3rd May 1980. Anfield, Liverpool 4 v Aston Villa 1, Graeme Souness and Terry McDermott toast their success

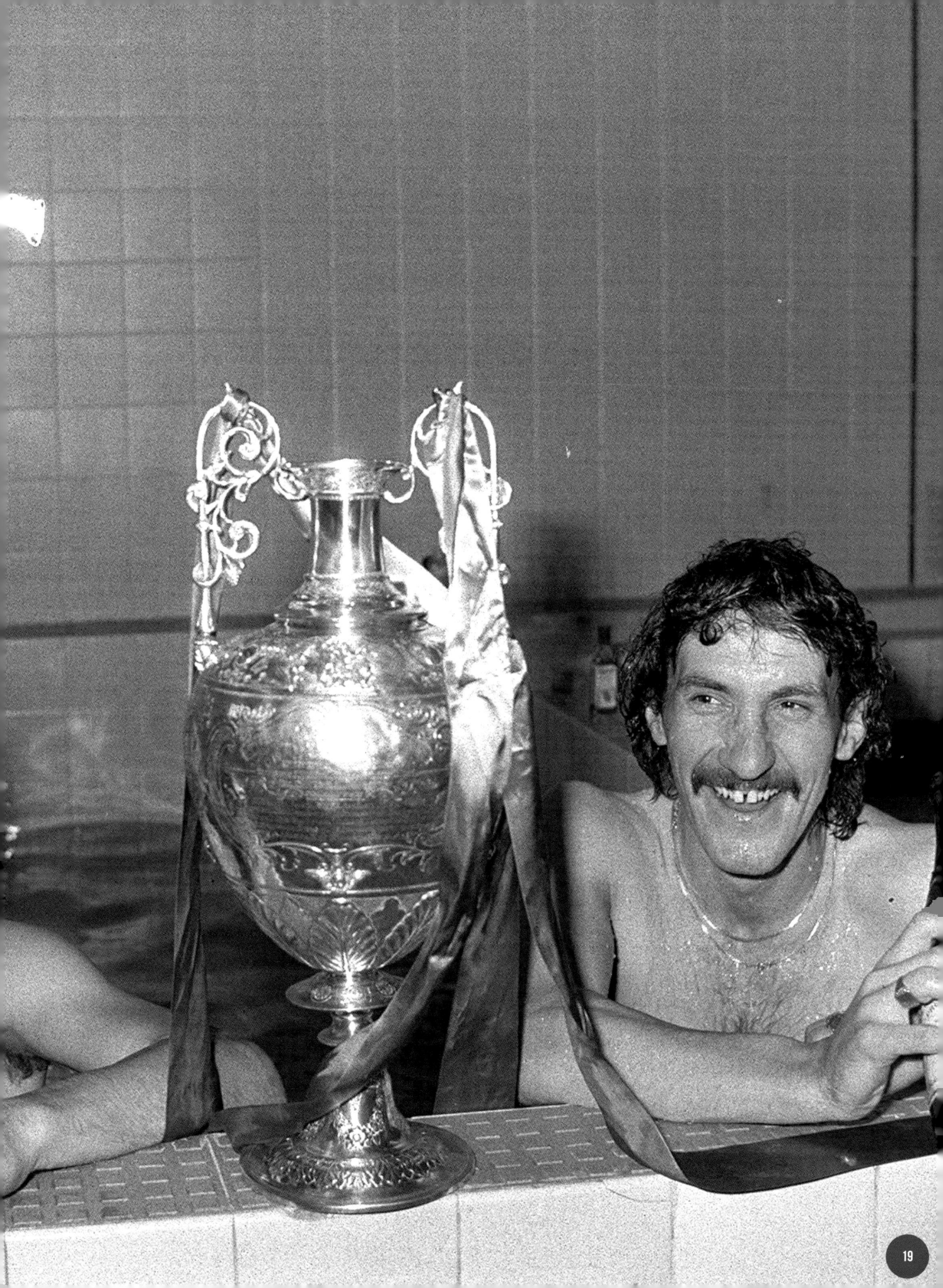

A CLASSIC MATCH MOMENT:

Undoubted winner this season came on the 8th of March 1980 when Terry McDermott scored in the FA Cup quarter-final against Tottenham Hotspur. Liverpool won 1-0 away from home when McDermott, outside the penalty area, calmly and cheekily chipped the ball into the air in front of himself before striking a volley over the heads of defenders and into the right-hand corner of the net. A superb goal from this superb player.

DERBY RESULTS:

TEAM	SCORE	TEAM	DATE
Liverpool	2-2	Everton	20th October 1979: Anfield
Everton	1-2	Liverpool	1st March 1980: Goodison Park.

PLAYER PROFILE:

TERRY McDERMOTT

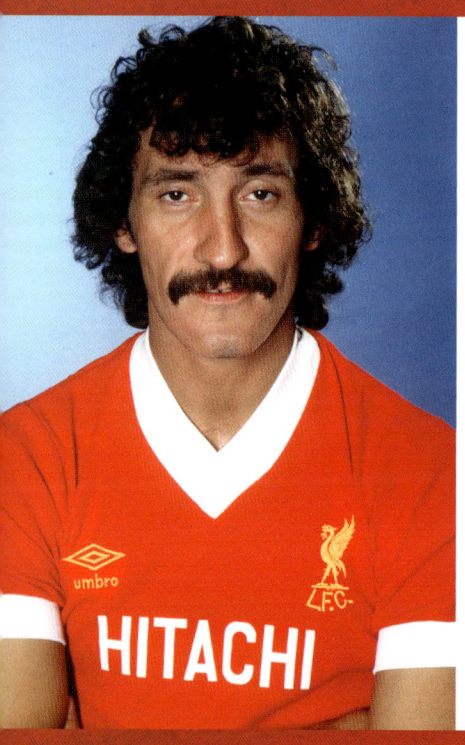

Terry McDermott was born in Liverpool on the 8th of December 1951. He joined Liverpool FC in 1974 under the management of Bob Paisley and played 329 games for the Reds scoring, 81 goals. His debut came on the 16th November 1974.

For the first two years, McDermott found it difficult to secure a regular first team slot, and by 1976, it seemed that he would decide to leave. He did not, and in 1977 began a career in midfield that would bring him spectacular results.

McDermott's games were filled with memorable goals, such as the one he scored against Tottenham in September 1978 when he hurtled 70 yards down the field to head home a Steve Heighway cross. His midfield artistry helped Liverpool win the League championship in 1977, the year he hit the goal of the season in the FA Cup semi-final against Everton. He also scored a hat trick against Hamburg in the second leg of Liverpool's victory in the 1977 UEFA Super Cup final.

In 1980 he was voted Player of the Year by both the Football Writers' Association and the Professional Footballers' Association. He was known as a quick-thinking, intelligent and instinctive player possessed of seemingly inexhaustible energy; at his best, Terry McDermott was considered one of the best strikers of the ball ever. Kenny Dalglish quipped that he must have had "... two pairs of lungs". His well-timed runs forward were the stuff of legend.

McDermott returned to Newcastle in 1982. He was capped for England 25 times. He has since been engaged at various clubs as assistant manager or coach.

McDermott has two sons, Neale and Gregg, and a daughter, Rachel.

MANAGER PROFILE:

BOB PAISLEY

Bob Paisley was born on the 23rd of January 1919 and died on the 14th of February 1996. Paisley took over as manager of Liverpool aged 55 when Bill Shankly retired in 1974. He joined Liverpool as a player in May 1939 and retired from playing in 1954 after 253 appearances when he became a physiotherapist for the club. Paisley was one of the original members of the "boot room", which was initiated by Bill Shankly as a place to discuss tactics.

Paisley, a man with a keen eye for talent, took over a Liverpool team that had been revitalised by Bill Shankly, but his own record was even better, and when he was in charge, Liverpool dominated English football. He led the team for nine seasons and he brought in at least one trophy for the club in eight of those. Paisley has managed 3 European Cup-winning sides; in 1977, 1978 and 1981. In 2012, this was still a record for any manager. Liverpool then also won the League title 6 times and won 3 League Cups, 5 Charity Shields and one European Super Cup. Paisley received the Manager of the Year award 6 times. By the time Bob Paisley retired in 1983 he had spent 44 years at the club. He then became a club director and right-hand man to Kenny Dalglish when Dalglish took over as manager.

Bob Paisley, the man who had to be almost forced to step into the limelight and was a Liverpool legend at the end of his career, was 77 when he died.

Bob Paisley proudly displays the League Championship Trophy

SNAKES AND LADDERS:
THE 1980/81 SEASON

his was Bob Paisley's 6th season in charge and he watched Liverpool play for a mighty double; the League Cup and the European Cup, to add to the Charity Shield, which the Reds claimed in August 1980 against West Ham United, 1-0.

In the league, Liverpool had what might be kindly described as an indifferent season characterised by a wodge of games in October 1980 that were all drawn back to back. After two successful seasons, this was a great disappointment all round. The team began well with a great 3-0 win against Crystal Palace and clouted West Bromwich 4-0 in September. They also brought home some high scoring wins against Brighton, 4-1, Manchester City, 3-0 and Middlesborough, 4-2, to land on second place. They hit top place in December after a 2-1 home win against Tottenham, so it all seemed to be coming together. Sadly, the promise was not fulfilled. It is an understatement to say that it was galling to lose to Everton in the fourth found of the FA Cup in January 1981, 1-2. And there was further pain on the 31st of the month; Liverpool's three-year, 85-match unbeaten home run record came to an end when they lost to Leicester City 2-1. Still, the boys were challenging throughout in the league and only lost the plot a little in March 1981. Then came five games without a win, including two losses, and they landed on eighth place, winning the final two games against Middlesborough and Manchester City to sneak back to fifth, the worst placing in ten years.

The derby match results only just turned in Liverpool's favour. Everton were marginally better placed at the end of the season than they had been in the 79/80 season, on 15th. In October 1980, the Reds could only manage a draw against Everton, 2-2 at Goodison. Come March 1981, the same month they had come away from Goodison Park with a 2-1 victory the year before, they went home from the Anfield game 1-0 victors. They were extremely lucky to win, because they didn't score; Everton's John Bailey did, in his own net after 77 goalless minutes. Better that than nothing …

But there was huge excitement anyway, because in May came the replay of the English League Cup final against West Ham United. The first game had resulted in a 1-1 draw, but:

Dalglish and Hansen – yes, you can't keep a good man back – hit the goals for the Reds that brought them the trophy in their second League Cup final.

And there was great European glory to play for one month later, because Liverpool had reached the final of the European Champions Cup against mighty Spanish club Real Madrid, having subdued Bayern Munich in the semi-final on away goals, 1-1, in Bavaria. A glorious achievement in itself. On the 27th of May 1980, the Reds held aloft the European Champions Cup having defeated the Spaniards 1-0. A sensational triumph made possible thanks to an Alan Kennedy goal in the 82nd minute.

9th August 1980. Liverpool celebrate with the Charity Shield

PLAYER DEBUTS

On the 13th of September 1980, Richard Money was given his head against West Bromwich Albion, and Howard Gayle, the first black player at Anfield, got his chance less than one month later on the 4th of October. Then came the man who was to make his own rules, Ian Rush, who started in the red shirt on the 13th of December against Ipswich Town. On the 14th of February 1981 it was Kevin Sheedy's turn against Birmingham, with a young, but soon to be a star, Ronnie Whelan playing against Stoke on the 3rd of April, and Colin Russell playing on the 2nd of May against Sunderland.

1st April 1981. Ian Rush holds aloft the League Cup trophy surrounded by fans

This season, Aston Villa, Ipswich Town, Arsenal and West Bromwich Albion were the ones to beat. Liverpool just squeaked into the top five ahead of Southampton and Nottingham Forest by one point,

and the final table looked like this:

POS	TEAM	POINTS	GD
1	Aston Villa	60	+32
2	Ipswich Town	56	+34
3	Arsenal	53	+16
4	West Brom	52	+18
5	Liverpool	51	+20

First up of the big four was West Bromwich Albion, who promptly collapsed 4-0 and gave Liverpool a boost to third place in the table. Ipswich could only manage a 1-1 draw at Anfield on October the 11th against the second-place Reds, and Arsenal had the same lack of luck at Anfield the following week. Ipswich got the same result, too, when they tried to crack the Red nut in Ipswich in December. In November, Aston Villa got singed at Anfield 2-1, so the first defeat amongst the big boys came on the 10th of January 1981 when Villa won a 2-0 victory at home and the Reds' downward slide began. In February 1981 came the next defeat; against West Bromwich, who won 2-0 at home. Another defeat, this time against Arsenal in March, 1-0, was the last of the games against the top four and dumped the Reds on 6th place. (They went as low as 8th, hitting 5th with the last game of the season.)

1981. Alan Hansen outjumps Ipswich Town's Clive Woods

THE STATISTICAL SEASON:

NUMBER OF GAMES:
Played	63
Won	31
Drawn	22
Lost	10

CLEAN SHEETS:
League	15
All Matches	24

GOALS SCORED:
League	62
All Matches	113

AVERAGE NUMBER OF GOALS SCORED IN EACH MATCH:
League	1.81
All Matches	2.52

AVERAGE NUMBER OF MINUTES REQUIRED FOR GOALS SCORED:
League	48
All Matches	49

AVERAGE HOME ATTENDANCE:
League	37,646
All Matches	35,912

CLASSIC MATCHES: 1980/81

LIVERPOOL V WEST BROMWICH ALBION, 4-0:
League Division One: Anfield, 13th September 1980.

West Bromwich eventually finished one place above Liverpool this season, so the win was as notable for the score line as for its importance. Liverpool were on fifth spot before this match and climbed to third after it.

As usual, the Reds played some wonderful flowing football with dream passes and skill on show, and came very close to scoring early on. Clemence was barely tested in the first half, which shows the stream of play was going Liverpool's way. Yet they couldn't make any of the attempts at goal count until the 27th minute. They were awarded a penalty when Robson did a brilliant left-handed save for West Bromwich after Fairclough's header almost reached the net. Unfortunately for West Brom, as Robson wasn't the West Bromwich keeper it was a penalty for the Reds. Robson was not booked, as he perhaps should have been, but Terry McDermott put the ball safely away, even though keeper Tony Godden got his hands to the ball.

Clemence was called upon for one of his magnificent leaping saves, following a West Bromwich free kick, but shortly after that, it was Souness in the 44th minute who popped in Liverpool's second. Dalglish had tricked the defence and sent a great pass through the West Bromwich defensive line to set up Souness, who tapped it with the side of his boot over the keeper. 2-0.

It was Dalglish again, having righted himself like lightning from a fall, who rounded a defender and set up Fairclough for his 67th minute goal, a beautiful flying header from Dalglish's cross. Fairclough's engagement meant that he was down for a few moments having hurt himself, but within four minutes he and Liverpool were back on the attack.

And what an attack it was, pass after pass moving forwards with a dummy thrown in for good measure. Cohen, Fairclough, McDermott. Fairclough got loose in the box and was spotted by Dalglish, who pushed the ball through, and the forward calmly slotted his second into the net past the keeper.

Liverpool didn't ease up and almost got a fifth. Only a terrific save by Godden stopped Lee's drive, and another headed attempt by Fairclough was kicked away.

All in all, a great display by the Reds.

1 Ray Clemence Goalkeeper
2 Phil Neal Defender
3 Avi Cohen Defender
4 Phil Thompson Midfielder
5 Ray Kennedy Defender
6 Alan Hansen Defender
7 Kenny Dalglish Forward
8 Sammy Lee Forward
9 David Fairclough Forward
10 Terry McDermott Midfielder
11 Graeme Souness Midfielder
12 Richard Money Defender

LIVERPOOL V WEST HAM 2-1:
English League Cup final: Villa Park, 1st April 1981

Liverpool had been almost home and dry in the League Cup final 18 days earlier when Alan Kennedy had put them into the lead, only to see West Ham draw level through a Ray Stewart penalty in extra time after McDermott had handled the ball.

Phil Thompson, who hadn't been fit to play in that first game and captained the team, was to describe Liverpool's play in this game as "brilliant". It was also the night when Ian Rush showed that his was an exceptional talent. "Even though he didn't score", said Thompson, "he was fantastic".

The night got off to a bad start though, when Paul Goddard scored a header for West Ham after just five minutes.

14th March 1981. League Cup Final, Wembley, Ray Kennedy takes on a trio of West Ham players

It took another twenty minutes of patient work by Liverpool before McDermott spotted Dalglish running in behind the defence and quick as a flash lobbed a superb, immaculately-calculated pass to his team mate, who volleyed the ball as he slid and scored the equaliser.

And then came the dream moment for everyone who loves Liverpool. Jimmy Case took a corner that curled over the West Ham box and a tall lean figure sailed up to head in the winning goal for the Reds. Alan Hansen had crept in and his header was deflected by Billy Bonds past the keeper Phil Parkes and into the net. That goal meant that the Reds had finally broken their bleak League Cup record and would take the trophy for the first time.

"We wanted to win it", recalled Thompson, "and it was a tremendous moment." There was so much revelry that they managed to leave the trophy on the back seat of the team bus! It was recovered next morning. A few embarrassed 'red' faces then!

1 **Ray Clemence** Goalkeeper
2 **Phil Neal** Defender
3 **Alan Kennedy** Defender
4 **Phil Thompson** Midfielder
5 **Ray Kennedy** Defender
6 **Alan Hansen** Defender
7 **Kenny Dalglish** Forward
8 **Sammy Lee** Forward
9 **Ian Rush** Forward
10 **Terry McDermott** Midfielder
11 **Jimmy Case** Midfielder
12 **Colin Irwin** Defender

BAYERN MUNICH V LIVERPOOL 1-1:
22nd April 1981: European Champions Cup Semi-Final: Olympiastadion, Munich

Liverpool met Bayern Munich again on the back of a goalless draw in the first game. The Reds' team was below strength. It was a tense night to say the least. Colin Irwin and Richard Money had little experience, but as it turned out they played the game of their lives. After the Reds had seen a nasty tackle put Dalglish out of the game, 19-year old Howard Gayle came on as a worthy substitute and he tore around the Bayern defence. It was a measure of his effectiveness that the only way he could be stopped was with a foul; he was taken down with a bad tackle inside the penalty box (but the referee did not award a penalty) and then again, for a free kick that McDermott put over the bar. Sadly, he was later booked for stupid foul on a German player. Gayle then left for the field for Jimmy Case to take over the job.

Liverpool had the best of the game, but Bayern began to put them under pressure in the second half and came very close to scoring.

Then Johnson played a one-touch volley to skipper Ray Kennedy in front of the German goal. Kennedy chested the ball down and hit it, before it touched the ground, wide of the German keeper to put the Reds in the lead with his 19th European goal. It was the 83rd minute.

Bayern now needed two goals to get through. A rare defensive lapse let Rummenigger loose, but his 87th minute equaliser came too late. Liverpool were into the final on an historic night.

1 **Ray Clemence** Goalkeeper
2 **Phil Neal** Defender
3 **Richard Money** Defender
4 **Colin Irwin** Midfielder
5 **Ray Kennedy** Defender
6 **Alan Hansen** Defender
7 **Kenny Dalglish** Forward
8 **Sammy Lee** Forward
9 **David Johnson** Forward
10 **Terry McDermott** Midfielder
11 **Graeme Souness** Midfielder
13 **Howard Gayle** Forward
12 **Steve Ogrizovic** Goalkeeper
16 **Avi Cohen** Defender
14 **Jimmy Case** Forward
13 **Howard Gayle** Forw/Midf/Wing
15 **Ian Rush** Forward

22nd April 1981. European Cup Semi - Final 2nd leg, Ray Clemence celebrates after Ray Kennedy's goal

LIVERPOOL V REAL MADRID 1-0:
27th May 1981 European Champions Cup Final: Parc des Princes, Paris

When Liverpool went to Paris they were certainly the underdogs. Liverpool, it was thought, were a team that had seen its best years. Little did anyone realise that a resurgence was under way and this game proved it beyond doubt. Although the match will not go down as a contender for a classic European Cup final, it was high in tension, skill and great teamwork.

Liverpool began by staking their claim, taking the game to their opponents and for twenty minutes caught the Spaniards on the wrong foot. Their characteristic swift, accurate passing served them well and calm appraisal of situations led to attempts at goal by the forwards with Alan Kennedy, McDermott and Dalglish.

Then the Spaniards got into gear and showed how dangerous they could be. It took all the professionalism and discipline of the defence to keep out Juanito, Cunningham and Santillana. The Spaniards skill on the ball was wonderful to watch and hard to contain as they burst into action from a slow build up, whilst the man-to-man marking they employed often made it difficult for them to restrict the likes of Dalglish. In this respect Camacho had a little more luck with Souness.

Liverpool still created more open chances to score, however, even if they could not recover their earlier dominance. The sides cancelled each other out with the result that everyone began to steel their nerves for extra time.

The 81st minute arrived and Liverpool had a throw-in. The ball fell to Alan Kennedy just outside the Real penalty area. Kennedy controlled the ball beautifully with his head, under pressure, ran through the defenders, pushed on towards the goal and fired a left-foot drive into the left-hand corner of the net past the approaching Real keeper. The ground erupted. It was a Liverpool moment to savour forever. Substitutions were made, Dalglish limped off and Jimmy Case took his place. And then it was over. Liverpool had taken the European Cup in a night of high excitement.

1 **Ray Clemence** Goalkeeper
2 **Phil Neal** Defender
3 **Alan Kennedy** Defender
4 **Phil Thompson** Midfielder
5 **Ray Kennedy** Defender
6 **Alan Hansen** Defender
7 **Kenny Dalglish** Forward
8 **Sammy Lee** Forward
9 **David Johnson** Forward
10 **Terry McDermott** Midfielder
11 **Graeme Souness** Midfielder
12 **Jimmy Case** Midfielder
13 **Steve Ogrizovic** Goalkeeper
14 **Colin Irwin** Defender
15 **Richard Money** Defender
16 **Howard Gayle** Forw/Wing/Midf

27th May 1981. Graeme Souness, Kenny Dalglish and Alan Hansen celebrate with the European Cup

A CLASSIC MATCH MOMENT:

Bayern Munich v Liverpool 1-1:
22nd April 1981: European Champions Cup Semi-Final: Olympiastadion, Munich
Ray Kennedy's drive, hit before it touched the ground, in the European Champions Cup semi-final.

DERBY RESULTS:

TEAM	SCORE	TEAM	DATE
Everton	2-2	Liverpool	18th October 1980: Goodison
Liverpool	1-0	Everton	21st March 1981: Anfield.

PLAYER PROFILE:
ALAN HANSEN ▼

Alan Hansen was born on the 13th of June 1955 in Sauchie, Scotland. He joined Liverpool in 1977 as a defender and stayed with the side throughout its great successes of the 70s and 80s, leaving in 1991 having played for the club 620 times. His debut came on the 24th of September 1977 against Derby County. He was good enough to impress one journalist who dubbed him the man of the match.

An accomplished sportsman, he also played golf, volleyball and squash to a high standard, Hansen was known for his cool-headed approach to the game, a vital character feature in a defender. His trademark was to smoothly run the ball forward and pass accurately to his forwards and midfielders rather than make long driving passes and even go so far forward that he scored 14 goals. Bob Paisley's heart was in his mouth whenever it happened, but Hansen knew what he was doing and his style contributed enormously to Liverpool's huge success; it was not unknown for him to save the day with a goal as he did against AZ Alkmaar in a 1981 European Cup tie. Hansen collected his first Football League Championship medal in 1979. He was also capped for Scotland 26 times.

In 1986, Hansen's hard work was rewarded with the team captaincy. After a knee injury kept him off the field for most of 1988/89, and he did not play at all in 1990/91, he announced his retirement in March 1991.

Not wishing to go into management, Hansen instead made a career for himself as a football commentator.

Hanson was considered to be one of the best footballers of his generation and one of the best defenders in the English league.

29th May 1981. The victorious Liverpool parade the European Cup on Merseyside

BACK TO THE TOP:
THE 1981/82 SEASON

Another superb season finished with the League Championship safely red-ribboned. It was the 13th league title. The FA Cup challenge was squashed in the fifth round, 2-0, by Chelsea, who were then in the Second Division; ask no questions...! And the European Cup challenge petered out in the quarter-finals when CSKA Sofia did the damage; 1-2 on aggregate after a first game won by Liverpool 1-0.

The league run could not have started off worse; there was just one win in the first four games to celebrate and two losses. The very first game was lost to Wolverhampton Wanderers 1-0. Indifferent form landed the Reds on 12th place after a 1-2 defeat by Manchester United at Anfield in October and they were back on 12th after a defeat to Manchester City in December. It wasn't looking good.

Then everything began to gel. There were just two more losses to endure until the end of the season and some wonderful scorelines; 4-0 against Notts County, Ipswich Town and Coventry and 5-1 against Stoke City, which was the first of a run of 16 games undefeated. By the beginning of April, Liverpool were on top of the table and there they stayed after thrashing Manchester City 5-0 and beating Manchester United 1-0.

25th May 1982. The team celebrate with the League Championship trophy

PLAYER DEBUTS

Three terrific players made their debuts simultaneously in the squad this season; on the 29th of August 1981, the inimitable keeper Bruce Grobbelaar played against Wolves, as did Craig Johnston and Mark Lawrenson.

> 13th March 1982. Mark Lawrenson in action against Tottenham's Chris Hughton

This was the year of the double derby victories and Everton went down 3-1 at Anfield and 3-1 at Goodison Park. No mistake, Liverpool were the better team this year.

This season, Ipswich were again challenging hard, with Manchester United not far behind, and two London clubs proved hard nuts to crack on home territory.

This is the table at the end of the season:

POS	TEAM	POINTS	GD
1	Liverpool	87	+48
2	Ipswich Town	83	+22
3	Man. United	78	+30
4	Tott. Hotspur	71	+19
5	Arsenal	71	+11

Arsenal limped home from a 2-0 defeat early in the season, but Ipswich were made of sterner stuff and Liverpool lost 2-0 away from home. Then came defeat to Manchester United at Anfield and that ghastly 12th place. In February 1982 it was Ipswich again, but the Reds were motoring hard by this time and their 4-0 victory must have come as a shock to the Ipswich side. Manchester United, too, got their comeuppance in April, beaten 1-0 at Old Trafford. Tottenham and Arsenal refused to be cowed, however, and took draws from their next clashes, before Tottenham went down 3-1 at Anfield in the penultimate game in May.

Tottenham already knew what Liverpool might do to them, because there had been a terrific victory in the League Cup, which fell to the Red onslaught in March 1982, as did Tottenham Hotspur, 3-1.

> 13th March 1982. Wembley, League Cup Final Bruce Grobbelaar celebrates victory

THE STATISTICAL SEASON:

NUMBER OF GAMES:

Played	62
Won	39
Drawn	13
Lost	10

CLEAN SHEETS:

League	20
All Matches	31

GOALS SCORED:

League	80
All Matches	129

AVERAGE NUMBER OF GOALS SCORED IN EACH MATCH:

League	1.86
All Matches	2.21

AVERAGE NUMBER OF MINUTES REQUIRED FOR GOALS SCORED:

League	51
All Matches	54

AVERAGE HOME ATTENDANCE:

League	35,213
All Matches	32,241

CLASSIC MATCHES: 1981/82

LIVERPOOL V AZ ALKMAAR, 3-2:
European Champions Cup: Anfield, 4th November 1981: R2, 2L

The two sides came together again after a 2-2 draw in Holland, when the Dutch side had fought back from 2 goals down. They gave Liverpool a hard time in the second game, too, with some swift ball play, and it was a close run thing until Alan Hansen decided to put an end to the agony.

Liverpool often played beautiful football and their cutting-edge passing almost put them ahead when both Dalglish and Souness sent the ball towards the goal. Souness struck a solid shot that bounced off the post and gave the Dutch a lucky escape.

Liverpool kept up the pressure, however, and the Dutch side finally ran out of luck. Three minutes before half time, Dalglish raced through the defence, chasing after a deflection. As Dalglish moved around the Dutch keeper – who had been left to face the Liverpool man alone – Treijtel seemed to take the striker's legs from under him. The penalty was awarded. McDermott stepped up and blasted the ball to the unhappy keeper's left and into the top of the net.

Ten minutes into the second half the Dutch threw a spanner in the works. It was their turn to apply pressure and after a lucky rebound had wrong-footed the defenders, the ball came to Keest Kist, who found himself with a clear view of the net and thumped a low drive across Grobbelaar and into the net.

Liverpool needed to drive their game forward, and the reward came in the 68th minute with a superb move that saw Dalglish cut through the Dutch defence and with a burst of speed, send the ball past the keeper to the centre of the goal, where Rush had slipped his marker, and he cracked the ball into the open goal.

The Dutch refused to give in and lady luck smiled on them again when Metjod lobbed a ball right over Grobbelaar's head. It hit the post and would have been made safe if the unlucky Thompson had not been directly beneath it. The ball came down from the woodwork, struck him, and bounced into the net. Back to square one for the Reds.

Now it was Liverpool's turn to retake the initiative. With five minutes to go, Liverpool were increasing the pressure and the attacks, and it was time for Alan Hansen to give poor Bob Paisley another heart attack by being where no defender is expected; in front of the opposition goal. McDermott's cross was helped into the air by a deflection, and Ronnie Whelan's back header found the lurking defender sandwiched between opposition defenders. But he fought his way out of the gridlock, sprinted forward and hit the ball as he fell, for the winning goal.

1 **Bruce Grobbelaar** Goalkeeper
2 **Phil Neal** Defender
3 **Mark Lawrenson** Defender
4 **Phil Thompson** Defender
5 **Ray Kennedy** Midfielder
6 **Alan Hansen** Defender
7 **Kenny Dalglish** Forward
8 **Ronnie Whelan** Midfielder
9 **Ian Rush** Forward
10 **Terry McDermott** Midfielder
11 **Graeme Souness** Midfielder
12 **Alan Kennedy** Defender
13 **Craig Johnston** Midfielder
14 **David Johnson** Forward
15 **Howard Gayle** Forw/Wing/Midf
16 **Steve Ogrizovic** Goalkeeper

LIVERPOOL V TOTTENHAM HOTSPUR, 3-1:
English League Cup: Wembley, 13th March 1982

This was to be Ronnie Whelan's hour of glory against a Tottenham side that boasted great players like Glenn Hoddle, Micky Hazard and Ossie Ardiles and, of course, Clemence in their squad. Unbeaten in 16 games, Spurs were confident that they could pull it off. And they came oh so very close. Archibald opened the scoring in the 11th minute for Tottenham after some clumsy defending by Liverpool, who had started well. For Liverpool, there now began almost 80 minutes of a Herculean battle, in which Souness fought like a tiger, to stay in the game.

4th November 1981. Ian Rush scores 2nd goal against AZ Alkmaar, European Cup 2nd round 2nd leg match

Liverpool never gave up and almost had the equaliser before half time. The chances came in the second half, too, and McDermott was unlucky not to score with a powerful drive.

Then Souness saved Liverpool as Tottenham drove forward to kill off the game, by kicking away a certain goal when Grobbelaar was off his line after a terrific save.

As the final three minutes began, it seemed that Spurs fans were going to be celebrating. Liverpool surged again, and it was one of those superb Liverpool passes that brought the Reds back to life – this one ran straight to the feet of Ronnie Whelan, who stabbed the ball fiercely past Clemence. After that, only a spectacular double save by Clemence from Rush rescued the game for Tottenham.

So extra time started, and the play flowed with excitement and near misses on both sides. On the 111st minute Liverpool began one of their swift passing attacks that put Dalglish clear in the Tottenham box and with a spot-on pass to Whelan, surrounded by Tottenham players in front of goal, the youngster put in his second. An astonishing Wembley debut for the Irishman. Then, after a Tottenham attack had been scuppered, came a brilliant long pass down the field by Sammy Lee to Ian Rush, who, after Johnston had almost lost the chance, took the ball back and in went the third. Liverpool had won the League Cup once more in what truly was, as Ronnie Whelan described it, "… a magical day".

1 **Bruce Grobbelaar** Goalkeeper
2 **Phil Neal** Defender
3 **Alan Kennedy** Defender
4 **Phil Thompson** Defender
5 **Ronnie Whelan** Midfielder
6 **Mark Lawrenson** Defender
7 **Kenny Dalglish** Forward
8 **Sammy Lee** Midfielder
9 **Ian Rush** Forward
10 **Terry McDermott** Midfielder
11 **Graeme Souness** Midfielder
12 **David Johnson** Forward

EVERTON V LIVERPOOL, 1-3:

League Division One: Goodison Park, 27th March 1982

Everton ran out for the derby unbeaten at home for 4 months, but it was Liverpool, without having been pressured too greatly, who went into the lead in the 21st minute. The Everton defence was split by pinpoint passing by Dalglish to Whelan, who was charging forward. Johnston's header from Whelan's cross tapped the bar, but when the ball came out to Whelan, he found himself unmarked in the confusion and drove home the first for Liverpool.

Everton went for a swift equaliser and Sharp was in place to get it just three minutes later after a corner caused uncharacteristic confusion in the Liverpool defence.

Rejuvenated, Everton tried to get ahead and almost succeeded, but Liverpool fought back and Alan Kennedy, on scintillating form, was almost the instigator of a wonderful goal when he tore past five Everton men to put Rush through, but the shot just went wide.

The opportunities at both ends continued to appear in the second half until a superb piece of football from Dalglish, holding off two Everton defenders in the penalty area, gave Souness, who was tearing in to help, the chance for a devastating drive that pounded into the Everton net. 57 minutes had passed.

Liverpool played some thrilling football, with passes that showed vision and accuracy almost taking the supporters' breath away. Still, the next goal would not come. Everton, however, were playing well and started to take control in the second half. Grobbelaar now showed what made him one of the best and kept the Blues out with some spectacular saves. Then, in the 81st minute, Liverpool fans could let the cheers rip when Craig Johnston was on the end of another delightful session of Liverpool passing, and his one-stop lob dropped into the net. A good game and terrific result that gained Liverpool one place in the table, moving them up to 3rd. Two weeks later they would be at the top.

1 **Bruce Grobbelaar** Goalkeeper
2 **Phil Neal** Defender
3 **Mark Lawrenson** Defender
4 **Alan Kennedy** Defender
5 **Ronnie Whelan** Midfielder
6 **Phil Thompson** Defender
7 **Kenny Dalglish** Forward
8 **Sammy Lee** Midfielder
9 **Ian Rush** Forward
10 **Craig Johnston** Midfielder
11 **Graeme Souness** Midfielder
12 **David Johnson** Forward

13th March 1982. Wembley, Ronnie Whelan celebrates scoring Liverpool's equalising goal against Spurs

A CLASSIC MATCH MOMENT:

Everton v Liverpool, 1-3:
League Division One: Goodison Park, 27th March 1982

Grobbelaar took off across his goalmouth when Everton's Sharp drove an unexpected thunderbolt in from outside the penalty area on the 27th March 1982 against Everton. Grobbelaar was in the air instantly and sailed up to the rising ball to snatch it out of the air. A superb save.

DERBY RESULTS:

TEAM	SCORE	TEAM	DATE
Liverpool	3-1	Everton	7th November 1981: Anfield.
Everton	1-0	Liverpool	27th March 1982: Goodison

PLAYER PROFILE:

IAN RUSH

Born on the 20th of November 1961 in Wales, Ian Rush made his Liverpool debut on the 13th of December 1980 in a 1-1 draw against Ipswich Town.

Rush was one of the top strikers in English football during the 1980s and 1990s and made 73 appearances for the Welsh national football team, where he remains top goalscorer with 28 goals. He also remains top goalscorer for Liverpool scoring 346 goals in all competitions for the Reds.

He has been voted PFA Young Player of the Year, PFA Players' Player of the Year and FWA Footballer of the Year 5 times; he was awarded the European Golden Boot in 1984 and the First Division Golden Boot the same year. He scored 3, 4 and 5 goals in individual games in that 1983/84 season scoring 47 goals in total. He was Liverpool's top goalscorer over eight seasons. He also holds the record for the most FA Cup final goals scored, having five to his credit and is the second top FA Cup competition scorer of all time, having the highest number in the 20th century; 44 goals.

After a slow build up at Anfield, Rush scored his first goal on the 30th of September 1981 in a European Cup tie, with his first league goals coming less than two weeks later, on the 10th October 1981, when Liverpool beat Leeds United 3-0. After that, Rush became an unstoppable goalscorer and put the ball into the net 30 times in 49 appearances in all competitions in the 1981/82 season.

Rush accepted an offer to leave Liverpool for Juventus on the 22nd July 1986.

He returned to Anfield after one season in Italy and stayed until 1996. In the 1989-90 season, Rush won his fifth and final League title, with Liverpool finishing nine points clear. In 1995 he gained his 5th League Cup winners' medal. He played his last game at Anfield on the 27th of April 1997 having appeared 660 times in red. The Ghost, as he was known for his stealth on the field, was, without doubt, one of Liverpool's greatest strikers.

13 March 1982. League Cup Final, Ronnie Whelan of Liverpool celebrates with Ian Rush and Alan Kennedy

THE END OF THE PAISLEY ERA:
THE 1982/83 SEASON

The second in the triplet of seasons of League Championship and League Cup doubles with the Charity Shield thrown in for good measure. This was an extraordinary season on several levels. The double, of course, is always extraordinary although Liverpool were beginning to make it seem otherwise. Liverpool won the Championship despite losing 5 of their last 7 games and drawing the other two. And the magnificent Bob Paisley announced that this was to be his last season in charge. The end of an incredible era indeed.

The Reds ran away with the title, which shows the magnitude of their dominance. They hit the top spot for the second time in October 1982 beating Brighton and Hove Albion 3-1 at Anfield, and there they stayed for the rest for the season. They notched up some classic wins; 5-0 against Southampton, and the killer 5-0 against Everton in the derby, in which Ian Rush scored 4 goals! This was Rush's second year as top goalscorer, a status he would eventually claim 8 times over his career. Fans could also enjoy the 4-0 against Coventry and 5-2 against Manchester City, followed up with 5-1 wins against both Notts. County and Stoke City. Watford were surging in the table, and they – alongside Nottingham Forest, Tottenham, Norwich City and Southampton – had revenge for an earlier defeat in that last string of lost matches; not that it mattered any longer by then.

Ah yes, the derbys. The second was a draw at Anfield 0-0. Och well, sometimes you just have to grin and bear it.

There was also the little matter of the European Cup that wasn't to be, after a 3-4 loss on aggregate to Widzew Lodz in March 1983. The FA Cup had slipped away, too, after a 5th round defeat to … Brighton and Hove Albion. Come on, you can't be serious, lads! Brighton came bottom of the table and were relegated, after all.

Good news. One week after that European defeat, Manchester United were skinned in the League Cup, and Liverpool retained the trophy.

Yes! Life was good in 1983!

August 1982. Kenny Dalglish in action during Charity Shield match

PLAYER DEBUTS

On the 21st of August 1982, David Hodgson was on the pitch against Tottenham, and ten days later on the 31st, it was Steve Nicol who got his first taste of Liverpool life.

◀ **23rd April 1983. David Hodgson in action against Norwich City**

The top four rivals were Watford, Manchester United, Tottenham and Nottingham Forest. Liverpool ran away from the top five, ahead of Watford by 11 points,

and the final table looked like this:

POS	TEAM	POINTS	GD
1	Liverpool	82	+50
2	Watford	71	+17
3	Man. United	70	+18
4	Tott. Hotspur	69	+15
5	Nott. Forest	69	+12

THE STATISTICAL SEASON:

NUMBER OF GAMES:

Played	60
Won	38
Drawn	10
Lost	12

CLEAN SHEETS:

League	19
All Matches	27

GOALS SCORED:

League	87
All Matches	120

AVERAGE NUMBER OF GOALS SCORED IN EACH MATCH:

League	2.62
All Matches	2.48

AVERAGE NUMBER OF MINUTES REQUIRED FOR GOALS SCORED:

League	50
All Matches	51

AVERAGE HOME ATTENDANCE:

League	34,836
All Matches	32,092

21st August 1982. Graeme Souness with the League Championship trophy ▶

CLASSIC MATCHES: 1982/83

LIVERPOOL V SOUTHAMPTON 5-0:
English League Division One: Anfield, 25th September 1982

A brief mention of another one of the many 5-0 victories that peppered the Liverpool score books over the years. Liverpool were unbeaten up to this point, and the game turned into the Whelan/Lawrenson show ... with Souness getting his nose in, too.

The show was up and running after only 6 minutes when Dalglish whizzed in and gave Whelan the chance to shoot. He did but was blocked, only to see the ball arc into the air over the keeper and into the net. Luck of the Irish as one commentator aptly put it. On his birthday, too. That was it for another 18 minutes. Then Dalglish set Souness up in space, and before Southampton knew what was happening, he had cracked the ball in past Shilton from far outside the penalty area.

Shilton was soon being severely tested by an avalanche of Liverpool shots, when Mark Lawrenson decided it should be a three-man show, on 41 minutes. He was sent away, sprinting almost the entire length of the Southampton half with the defenders left floundering, to finally slide it past Shilton.

The next Lawrenson goal, which came on the 67th minute, was the result of a magnificent piece of teamwork. Lawrenson began the run forward with the ball, pushed it to Johnston, who, with a great sense of where his teammates were, dummied and let the ball roll to Dalglish. He sent it on back into the path of Lawrenson at the end of his run, and Lawrenson pushed it in under Shilton, just as he had his first goal.

At this point, Ronnie Whelan thought that he might put the icing on the cake. 71 minutes and Johnston went through and around Shilton, although the keeper blocked his first cross attempt. His second was pounced on by Whelan with the defence left ogling, and in went the 5th, the last goal in a wonderful afternoon of Liverpool craftsmanship.

1 Bruce Grobbelaar Goalkeeper
2 Phil Neal Defender
3 Alan Kennedy Defender
4 Phil Thompson Defender
5 Ronnie Whelan Midfielder
6 Mark Lawrenson Defender
7 Kenny Dalglish Forward
8 Sammy Lee Midfielder
9 Ian Rush Forward
10 Craig Johnston Midfielder
11 Graeme Souness Midfielder
12 Terry McDermott Forward

EVERTON V LIVERPOOL, 0-5:
English League Division One: Goodison Park, 6th November 1982

This just had to be included from this season! It was as though every fan's glorious dream had come true. Liverpool were already on the top spot when they went to Everton and as we have just read, they had lashed Southampton the same way in September. But Everton? Ian Rush was a one-man blue destruction event, and he opened the show after just 11 minutes of play. It was Hansen, giving Paisley yet another heart attack, who took the ball from Everton, rounded a defender, ran forward and at speed slid a perfect pass through two defenders to Rush, whose first-time strike landed in the net. Liverpool play at its finest.

Rush hit the bar after another defence-splitting through ball and Everton could not get into their stride against the revolving Reds, who could have put in several more goals before half time; apart from off-target shots, Rush and Lee were unlucky to hit the woodwork, and Dalglish had a goal disallowed.

In the second half, Liverpool found the gear stick and went into overdrive, playing the slick, flowing football that won trophies. Within ten minutes, Ian Rush had scored again from the edge of the penalty area, and then Mark Lawrenson had a go on 55 minutes.

Rush scored his hat trick in the 71st minute with a charge into the Everton half from the half way line and

1983. Bruce Grobbelaar clowning around during a training session at Melwood, Liverpool

having beaten Everton keeper Southall, watched the ball rebound from the post. He then calmly re-struck the ball to claim his goal.

Fourteen minutes later, he repeated the trick and this time made no mistake, gliding past the keeper to make history with his fourth goal. An extraordinary performance from Rush and the team, and a joy for anyone lucky enough to have witnessed it.

1 Bruce Grobbelaar Goalkeeper
2 Phil Neal Defender
3 Alan Kennedy Defender
4 Phil Thompson Defender
5 Craig Johnston Midfielder
6 Alan Hansen Defender
7 Kenny Dalglish Forward
8 Sammy Lee Midfielder
9 Ian Rush Forward
10 Mark Lawrenson Defender
11 Graeme Souness Midfielder
12 David Hodgson Forward

LIVERPOOL V MANCHESTER UNITED, 2-1:

League Cup Final: Wembley, 26th March 1983

What a crackling nail biter this turned out to be! Bob Paisley was in charge for his last game, so emotions were high, the boys wanting to bag this one as a tribute to the boss. The clubs had met and drawn in previous matches this season; it was anyone's guess what would happen.

United seemed to have wrapped it up after 12 minutes with a terrific goal from 17-year old Norman Whiteside, who evaded Hansen to strike from the edge of the penalty area.

Liverpool did not yield an inch, however, and as the Daily Mail said, the "… midfield four of Souness, Whelan, Lee and Johnston were faultless". Liverpool went on the search for the equaliser, pressurising their rivals constantly and were extremely dangerous. Manchester thought they could wait out the whistle and eventually paid the price. Liverpool moved swiftly but patiently and when Kennedy struck in the 75th minute after another sharp Liverpool build-up it was no less than the Reds deserved. It was a beauty of a shot from well outside the penalty area on the left-hand side, right across the goalmouth and the keeper and into the far corner of the net.

Liverpool did well to keep out United, with Grobbelaar 25 yards out of goal to stop a United attack on one occasion and booked for bringing down United's McQueen in doing so. But he might just have saved the day for Liverpool when they failed to capitalise on some good chances, which was, in fact, the complaint of the day.

Still, in extra time Liverpool were playing well, and there was a touch of magic on the 99th minute when Ronnie Whelan scored a wonderful winner. As the Reds surged into the box, Whelan's attempt at a through pass was blocked, so when the ball came back to him he cheekily drove a curving ball into the air, which sailed into the net.

United were always dangerous but failed to take their own chances. Fairclough missed three with clear shots at goal, and Liverpool were at risk of the Manchester side's attacks.

But Liverpool won the day and the League Cup for the third year in a row. A magnificent game and achievement. What a way for Bob Paisley to hand over the reigns.

1 Bruce Grobbelaar Goalkeeper
2 Phil Neal Defender
3 Alan Kennedy Defender
4 Mark Lawrenson Defender
5 Ronnie Whelan Midfielder
6 Alan Hansen Defender
7 Kenny Dalglish Forward
8 Sammy Lee Midfielder
9 Ian Rush Forward
10 Craig Johnston Midfielder
11 Graeme Souness Midfielder
12 David Fairclough Forward

26th March 1983. Milk Cup Final, Graeme Souness commits to a tackle from behind on Norman Whiteside

A CLASSIC MATCH MOMENT:

Liverpool v Manchester United, 2-1
English League Cup: Wembley, 26th March 1983.
That skillful and confident Ronnie Whelan winner that curved into the air and sailed majestically into the net.

DERBY RESULTS:

TEAM	SCORE	TEAM	DATE
Everton	0-5	Liverpool	6th November 1982: Goodison
Liverpool	0-0	Everton	19th March 1983: Anfield

PLAYER PROFILE: KENNY DALGLISH ▼

Kenneth Dalglish was born in Glasgow on the 4th of March 1951. In a career that lasted 22 years, he won the Ballon d'Or Silver Award as well as PFA Player of the Year In 1983. He received the FWA Footballer of the Year in 1979 and 1983, and in 2009, Four Four Two named him as the greatest striker in post-war football in Britain. In 2006 he came top of the Liverpool fans' "100 Players Who Shook the Kop" poll, and he has been inducted into both the English and Scottish Football Halls of Fame.

"… Dalglish wants to get on, but I would have moved heaven and earth to keep him. I would rather have quit and got out of the game altogether than sold a player of his brilliance." These were Bill Shankly's words when he heard that Dalglish was coming to Liverpool and showed the esteem in which Dalglish was held in the football world.

Dalglish played his first match for Liverpool on the 13th August 1977 in a 0-0 draw against Manchester United. His first League goal came one week later against Middlesbrough and he finished the first season at Liverpool with 31 goals to his credit and had also scored the winning goal against Bruges in the 1978 European Cup final.

The following season he was named Football Writers Association Footballer of the Year.

Dalglish became manager of Liverpool when Joe Fagan retired in 1985, to become the first player-manager in English football. He became one of Liverpool's most successful managers and as a player, scored the winning goal against Chelsea to give Liverpool their 16th League title.

He made 515 appearances for Liverpool, playing his last match on the 1st May 1990 having scored 172 goals for the club.

7th May 1983. Bob Paisley, surrounded by his players, holds the First Divison Championship Trophy

GOOD THINGS COME IN THREES:
THE 1983/84 SEASON

A season of superlatives that would see Ian Rush score more goals than ever before to end his third season in a row as top goalscorer, on 47. A season that brought Joe Fagan from assistant manager to the manager seat for the next two years, and the season that brought an incredible triple with the 15th League Championship, the League Cup and the European Cup flying red ribbons. It was the third consecutive league and League Cup-winning season.

It was to be the last season for a Liverpool legend, that rock in midfield, Graeme Souness, who then left England for Italy and Sampdoria. It was also the season in which Kenny Dalglish scored his 100th league goal, on the 26th November against Ipswich, and then had his cheekbone broken in a match against Manchester United in the new year.

The elusive FA Cup proved as slippery as ever and Brighton and Hove Albion, not even in the First Division now, put the knife in, in the fourth round. Ugh. Must be the south sea air.

The season began with a loss – perhaps they all should, considering how it continued! Liverpool lost to Manchester United 2-0 in the Charity Shield game in August 1983, so United must have fancied their chances that year. They had to think again.

Six games, four victories, no defeats was the tally before another loss to United at Old Trafford, 1-0. That dropped the Reds to 6th place. They recovered swiftly, though, and by the time they lost again, to Coventry in December, 4-0 – yes, the same Coventry that finished 19th in the table – Liverpool were on top of the table with a 6-0 belting of Luton behind them. (And a 6-0 belting of West Ham still to come!) They didn't leave that position and took the 15th title despite winning just 2 of the final 8 games. Coventry were made to pay for the earlier humiliation with a 5-0 hammering, though!

United were hot contenders throughout the season, but it was Southampton who snapped at the Reds' heels on second place and Nottingham Forest likewise, with Queens Park Rangers just one point behind United. This was the final table:

27th August 1984 Kenny Dalglish in action against Wolves

PLAYER DEBUTS

Michael Robinson arrived in August 1983 from Brighton and Hove Albion to play his first game for Liverpool, against Manchester United, on the 20th of that month. On the 7th of February 1984, Gary Gillespie, bought from Coventry City, played against Walsall, and John Wark had his first red experience on the 31st March 1984 against Watford; Wark scored in his debut at Vicarage Road in a 2-0 win (and also scored at Anfield against Watford in 1985).

◀ **31st March 1984. John Wark shields the ball from Watford's John Barnes**

POS	TEAM	POINTS	GD
1	Liverpool	80	+41
2	Southampton	77	+28
3	Nott. Forest	74	+31
4	Man. United	74	+30
5	QPR	73	+30

The first test was against Nottingham Forest in September 1983 at Anfield, which brought a 1-0 victory for Liverpool. In December Liverpool had the same result at Nottingham's City Ground. Next of the big boys was Southampton also in September; 1-1 at Anfield, and Liverpool were on 5th place in the league. Later in the month, Manchester did the dirty at Old Trafford, 1-0. Then came QPR, who went down 1-0 in October. In January, Manchester United took a draw, 1-1, from Anfield, where in February 1984, QPR lost 2-0. The last of the big games came in March 1984 and a 2-0 loss to Southampton, which might have proved fatal in the light of five drawn games up until the end of the season.

20th August 1983. FA Charity Shield, Ronnie Whelan volleys the ball ▲

THE STATISTICAL SEASON:

NUMBER OF GAMES:
Played	67
Won	37
Drawn	22
Lost	08

CLEAN SHEETS:
League	20
All Matches	34

GOALS SCORED:
League	73
All Matches	118

AVERAGE NUMBER OF GOALS SCORED IN EACH MATCH:
League	2.38
All Matches	2.39

AVERAGE NUMBER OF MINUTES REQUIRED FOR GOALS SCORED:
League	46
All Matches	47

AVERAGE HOME ATTENDANCE:
League	32,021
All Matches	30,290

CLASSIC MATCHES: 1983/84

ASTON VILLA V LIVERPOOL 1-3:

League Division One, 20th January 1984

Another triumph, with Ian Rush at his sizzling best netting another hat trick. Wearing yellow kit, Liverpool went to Villa Park on the back of a home defeat against Wolverhampton the week before, so they needed to get stuck in. But they made hard work of the first half and paid for it by going down to a Dennis Mortimer goal just 15 minutes in, after the defence had been split by a slick through pass. Liverpool slowly came back into the game, but it was 1-0 at half time.

Liverpool were still inconsistent after the break although Rush had begun the destruction in the first minute, taking a long pass and driving the ball low into the net. Villa pressed forward, and it could have gone either way, until Rush was on the spot again on the 70th minute scoring a magnificent goal with a volley from a Steve Nicol header that had flown high into the air and dropped in front of him.

Rush followed that with his hat trick on the 80th minute. Nicol lobbed the ball to him over a defender, who couldn't quite control the situation, and Rush pounced to send an immaculate lob over the keeper. His fingers touched the ball but could not stop it dropping into the net. And so another Ian Rush show came to end.

1 Bruce Grobbelaar Goalkeeper
2 Phil Neal Defender
3 Alan Kennedy Defender
4 Mark Lawrenson Defender
5 Steve Nicol Midfielder
6 Alan Hansen Defender
7 Michael Robinson Forward
8 Sammy Lee Midfielder
9 Ian Rush Forward
10 Craig Johnston Midfielder
11 Graeme Souness Midfielder
12 Ronnie Whelan Midfielder

LIVERPOOL V EVERTON 1-0:

English League Cup Final Replay: Maine Road, 28th March 1984

Well what do you know, it's another classic against Everton!

This clash of the Liverpudlians was the replay of the Wembley game that had ended in a draw; only just, after a controversial goal-line clearance by Hansen. In what was described as a "... constant, non-stop battle", Graeme Souness was in red for the last time in a League Cup final. And it was his presence that made the difference as Everton brought the game to the Liverpool defenders and could have taken the honours on a variety of occasions. Liverpool was a team that did not perform at its best in the first half. Reid and Richardson were only just denied glory. Not only was Souness the rock in the storm of the defence, he was there on the 21st minute, albeit with his back to the goal, when, as he put it later, he "... flashed a leg at it and it just dipped in front of Everton keeper Neville Southall before going in". It was lucky he flashed that leg, because Liverpool were far from being in command. As the second half wore away, Everton began to sense the chance slipping away and let themselves open to the dangerous Liverpool forwards. Liverpool had chances to secure the game, but failed to take them and instead the tension increased as Everton tried to equalise, with Reid an ever-present danger to the Liverpool goal.

All to no avail, Liverpool held on to take the trophy for the fourth consecutive year and give Joe Fagan his first trophy as manager.

1 Bruce Grobbelaar Goalkeeper
2 Phil Neal Defender
3 Alan Kennedy Defender
4 Mark Lawrenson Defender
5 Ronnie Whelan Midfielder
6 Alan Hansen Defender
7 Kenny Dalglish Forward
8 Sammy Lee Midfielder
9 Ian Rush Forward
10 Craig Johnston Midfielder
11 Graeme Souness Midfielder
12 Michael Robinson Forward

28th March 1984. Bruce Grobbelaar commands the air above Everton striker Adrian Heath

30th June 1984. Liverpool Lineup for the European Cup Final

LIVERPOOL V ROMA 1-1
AET: LIVERPOOL WON 4-2 ON PENALTIES:
European Champions Cup Final: Stadio Olimpico, 30th May 1984

Liverpool arrived in the Stadio Olimpico in Rome with a string of impressive victories under their belts against Odensee, (6-0) Bilbao, (1-0) Benfica (5-1) and Dinamo Bucharest (3-1).

Unfortunately, the hoped-for clash of titans turned into a midfield power struggle that left the forwards on both sides with little to latch on to.

After some dangerous moments for Liverpool, it was the Reds who changed the game's dynamic when they snatched a 15th-minute goal. Johnston got the ball after a move begun by Souness and Lee. Johnston's cross sailed over to Whelan at the far post. Then a scramble in front of the goalmouth began when Whelan and the Italian goalkeeper bumped into one another and the ball dropped to Rush, who couldn't quite make it happen. The attempted clearance was blocked and shot across the goalmouth again where Neal picked it up and calmly slotted home the goal between two defenders.

Liverpool might have had two more, but a disallowed Souness goal and a saved Rush drive let the Italians breath again.

Just before half-time, a Conti cross reached Pruzzo's head, and the lovely header arced over Grobbelaar into the net. The game was wide open again.

The second half was filled with caution as was extra time, and both sides had their keepers to thank that they did not go behind.

So it came down to a nail-biting penalty shoot out. Made worse when Nicol missed the first penalty, nervously sending the ball high into the air. Di Bartolomei cracked his shot in, as did Phil Neal, and Liverpool hearts jumped when Conti misfired and sent the ball over the bar. Souness whacked his into the top corner, Righetti side-footed his in, and Rush slipped his in beautifully, so it was up to Graziani to keep his side on course. He missed, the ball sailing high, hitting the bar and off into the air to the joy of Grobbelaar. The weight of the world was on Kennedy as he stepped up and fired the ball in, instantly achieving hero status. Liverpool had lifted the European Cup for the fourth time.

1 Bruce Grobbelaar Goalkeeper
2 Phil Neal Defender
3 Alan Kennedy Defender
4 Mark Lawrenson Defender
5 Ronnie Whelan Midfielder
6 Alan Hansen Defender
7 Kenny Dalglish Forward
8 Sammy Lee Midfielder
9 Ian Rush Forward
10 Craig Johnston Midfielder
11 Graeme Souness Midfielder
12 Michael Robinson Forward
13 Bob Bolder Goalkeeper
14 Steve Nicol Midfielder
15 David Hodgson Forward
16 Gary Gillespie Defender

30th June 1984. Liverpool celebrate with the European Cup

A CLASSIC MATCH MOMENT:

Aston Villa v Liverpool, 1-3

League Division One, 20th January 1984

That man Rush scored a gorgeous 70th minute goal when a Steve Nicol header flew high into the air and dropped in front of him. The volley was a joy to behold.

DERBY RESULTS:

TEAM	SCORE	TEAM	DATE
Liverpool	3-0	Everton	7th November 1981: Anfield.
Everton	1-1	Liverpool	27th March 1982: Goodison
Liverpool	0-0	Everton	25th March 1984: Wembley; League Cup Final
Liverpool	1-0	Everton	28th March 1984: Maine Road; League Cup Final Replay

PLAYER PROFILE: GRAEME SOUNESS

Born on the 6th of May 1953 in Edinburgh, Scotland, Souness came to Liverpool in 1978 from Middlesborough, and the man who was to be undisputed king of the midfield formed a formidable triumvirate with Dalglish and Hansen, and took over the captaincy at Christmas 1981. During his time at Liverpool he won five League Championships, three European Cups and four League Cups.

His skill in midfield, not forgetting the vital goals he often scored, 55 in all, made him a star midfielder of his generation and he was capped 54 times for Scotland.

He left Liverpool after 359 games for the Reds with his final appearance (and goal) coming in the European Cup Final on May 5th 1984 against Roma.

Souness then went to Sampdoria in Italy, and after that he joined Rangers as player-manager.

Souness returned to Liverpool as their manager between 1991 and 1994. His time as manager was fraught with problems; an aging team that reacted adversely to his strict training style was one of the greatest. He underwent major heart surgery in 1992.

After Liverpool, Souness went to Galatasaray in Turkey.

He has been married twice, first to Danielle Wilson and then to Karen with whom he lives in Dorset.

In 2007 he was inducted into the English Football Hall of Fame. He is also in the Rangers' Hall of Fame.

MANAGER PROFILE: JOE FAGAN

Joe Fagan was born on the 12th of March 1921 in Liverpool and died on the 30th June 2001 in Liverpool aged 80. He took charge of his first game on 20th of August 1983 when Liverpool lost 0-2 against Manchester United in the Charity Shield.

Fagan played wing-half with Manchester City and came to Liverpool on June 30th 1958 as a coach. He took over as first team trainer in July 1974 following Bill Shankly's departure, and became Bob Paisley's right-hand man. Legend has it that he created the famous 'Boot Room' where Shankly would hold meetings to discuss strategy, tactics, players etc.

Graeme Souness remembers that Fagan's takeover was seamless and easy, as Fagan was steeped in Paisley's management style. As manager of Liverpool, Fagan became the first British football manager to win three major titles in one season, claiming the League Cup, the League Championship and the European Cup. The Reds were second in the league during his next year in charge and just missed out on the other big trophies. Fagan's announcement that he was going to retire came just before Liverpool were about to play Juventus in the European Cup final in 1985. The trauma of the Heysel Stadium disaster never left him and affected him badly.

Fagan received the English Manager of the Year award in 1984.

THE ONE THAT GOT AWAY: THE 1984/85 SEASON

A year never to be forgotten that is indelibly marked as the year the Heysel Stadium tragedy occurred in the European Cup Final in Brussels, Belgium. 39 Juventus fans died. Joe Fagan had announced his retirement just hours before the match after a season of mighty disappointments, and the 1-0 loss to Juventus crowned the lot. Or perhaps losing the league title to Everton did that. It was a pretty horrible season altogether that included a run of 7 games without a win starting with a 1-3 loss to Arsenal in the 5th game of the season. At one point, the Reds were on 17th place, even harder to stomach because Everton put them there after a 0-1 defeat at Anfield in October 1984. The Reds recovered to claw their way back up the table, but it took them until May 1985 to get there and they were 13 points adrift of their blue rivals by that time.

That meant that Everton had beaten Liverpool three times because they had also taken the Charity Shield 1-0, and Tottenham had bounced them out of the League Cup, 1-0, Manchester United did the honours in the FA Cup after a semi-final replay in April; 4-3 on aggregate.

By the time the European Cup Final came around, Juventus had already pushed the Reds out of the UEFA Super Cup with a 2-0 win in January 1985. John Wark was top goalscorer of the season with just 27 goals; it was plain that this had not been a good year.

December 1984. Liverpool training session in Tokyo

PLAYER DEBUTS

Two classic newbies this season. But what a year to start in red as Paul Walsh did against Everton in the Charity Shield on the 8th of August 1984, and the Danish player Jan Mølby on the 25th August against Norwich City. Mølby eventually spent 12 years at the club. On the 10th of November 1984 it was Jim Beglin's turn. He started against Southampton in a 1-1 draw. Finally Kevin MacDonald went out against Luton Town on the 29th of December 1984. At least he was part of a winning side in his debut, 1-0.

◀ **August 1985. Jan Molby of Liverpool in action against Newcastle United at St James' Park**

Liverpool struggled against all the top clubs in the league this season. Chelsea and Arsenal just failed to make the top five.

This was the final table:

POS	TEAM	POINTS	GD
1	Everton	90	+45
2	Liverpool	77	+33
3	Tott. Hotspur	77	+27
4	Man. United	76	+30
5	Southampton	68	+09

First to come along was Manchester United in September 1984. That was a 1-1 draw at Old Trafford, which was comforting. The 1-0 defeat at White Hart Lane to Tottenham Hotspur in October was certainly not. Nor was the 0-1 loss to Everton at Anfield. A 1-1 draw was all that could be managed against Southampton at Anfield in November. Then two terrible matches; Tottenham came to Anfield in March and promptly put a spanner in the works with a 1-0 win. Manchester United threw in another for good measure at the end of the month. Southampton also repeated their earlier cold sponge act with a 1-1 draw in May, and a fairly miserable season ended with a 0-1 defeat to Everton at Goodison Park.

16th January 1985. European SuperCup, Turin, Kevin MacDonald points an accusing finger at Antonio Cabrini ▲

THE STATISTICAL SEASON:

NUMBER OF GAMES:

Played	64
Won	33
Drawn	15
Lost	16

CLEAN SHEETS:

League	19
All Matches	29

GOALS SCORED:

League	68
All Matches	107

AVERAGE NUMBER OF GOALS SCORED IN EACH MATCH:

League	1.71
All Matches	2.21

AVERAGE NUMBER OF MINUTES REQUIRED FOR GOALS SCORED:

League	51
All Matches	54

AVERAGE HOME ATTENDANCE:

League	34,465
All Matches	33,348

CLASSIC MATCHES: 1984/85

LIVERPOOL V BENFICA 3-1:
European Champions Cup: Anfield, 24th October 1984

Another one-man sharpshooting show from the mighty Ian Rush against lofty Benfica. Rush was recovering from a cartilage injury, and the team as a whole was having to deal with injury problems. Also, Liverpool were suffering from the departure of Souness, and the attacks were no longer as smooth as they been when the Scotsman was the boss.

It was an uneven game for the Reds; Dalglish was certainly the man who kept the team in the game, feeding his team mates and almost scoring himself. Nonetheless, it was Rush who got the first, on the 44th minute, after Lawrenson had charged up into the Benfica box past three defenders, and his cross had gone to Wark, who gave it to Rush and in it went.

It was lack of urgency and a slip on the wet grass by Gillespie that let the Portuguese Diamantino through for a terrific equaliser in the 52nd minute. It seemed that Liverpool would now be in severe trouble.

Not so. For on the 71st, minute Rush struck again when a weak shot by Whelan was given more force and redirected by the number 9 into the Benfica goal. Bento had to retrieve the ball from his net once more in the 76th minute. With water lying on the pitch, Liverpool caused trouble in the Benfica box, and a rebound came to Rush. He immediately had it in the net for his hat trick. In a season of disappointments, this game stands out as a hard-won victory.

1 Bruce Grobbelaar Goalkeeper
2 Phil Neal Defender
3 Alan Kennedy Defender
4 Mark Lawrenson Defender
5 Ronnie Whelan Midfielder
6 Alan Hansen Defender
7 Kenny Dalglish Forward
8 Sammy Lee Midfielder
9 Ian Rush Forward
10 John Wark Midfielder
11 Gary Gillespie Defender
12 Craig Johnston Midfielder
13 Bob Bolder Goalkeeper
14 Jim Beglin Defender
15 Phil Thompson Defender
16 Michael Robinson Forward

LIVERPOOL V PANATHINAIKOS 4-0:
European Champions Cup: Anfield, 10th April 1985. Semi-final, 1L

Liverpool showed that they could be champions again in what was described as a 'masterclass' in the game of football. They pressurised the Greeks in their green kit, constantly forcing them into mistakes. Yet the Reds had to wait for over half an hour to show that they were truly in charge. The Greeks even had a goal disallowed shortly after Rush had muffed a chance that he would usually put in with one foot tied behind his back. Full credit goes to Greek defender Mavridis, who tied down Rush throughout the first half.

It was a Wark goal that gave the Reds the starting gun to run amok, after his 23rd goal in European competitions. It came in the 35th minute when MacDonald's drive bounced off the post, and the hovering Wark caught the defence napping, ran in to pick up the rebound and thumped in the opening goal, wide of the keeper.

In the second half, Liverpool came out in confident mood and were soon pressing down on the Greeks.

Then Liverpool began another of their immaculate quick-passing attacks that ended in a great cross by Whelan to Rush, whose header went in from close range. And now that he was released, Rush darted forward 2 minutes later leaving the defenders behind him to put in his second from a long pass by Lee, on the 50 minutes mark.

Thirty-five minutes on from that goal, Beglin, who had been having a terrific game, got his just rewards. He came hurtling into the box unseen by the Greek defenders, rising upwards to meet a beautifully weighted free kick by Dalglish and sending a cracking header into the net for number 4.

1 Bruce Grobbelaar Goalkeeper
2 Phil Neal Defender
3 Jim Beglin Defender
4 Mark Lawrenson Defender
5 Sammy Lee Midfielder
6 Alan Hansen Defender
7 Kenny Dalglish Forward
8 Ronnie Whelan Midfielder
9 Ian Rush Forward
10 Kevin MacDonald Midfielder
11 John Wark Midfielder
12 Gary Gillespie Defender
13 Bob Bolder Goalkeeper
14 Jan Mølby Midfielder
15 Craig Johnston Midfielder
16 Paul Walsh Forward

10th April 1985. Alan Hansen challenges Panathinaikos defender Nicos Karoulias

24th October 1984. Ian Rush is congratulated by Ronnie Whelan and John Wark after scoring during the Liverpool v Benfica European Cup 2nd Round 1st leg match at Anfield

A CLASSIC MATCH MOMENT:

Liverpool v Panathinaikos 4-0
European Champions Cup: Anfield, 10th April 1985. Semi-final, 1L.
Beglin's goal was a cracker, and he had been having a great game anyway. He timed his run into the box perfectly, unnoticed by the Greek defenders and powered a cracking header into the net for number 4.

DERBY RESULTS:

TEAM	SCORE	TEAM	DATE
Liverpool	0-1	Everton	18th August 1984: Wembley
Liverpool	0-1	Everton	20th October 1984: Anfield
Everton	1-0	Liverpool	23rd May 1985: Goodison

PLAYER PROFILE:

PHIL NEAL ▼

Phil Neal was born in Irchester, Northamptonshire on the 20th of February 1951 and began his career at Liverpool in 1974 becoming one of the most successful players there and in English football. He won the First Division championship eight times and also four League Cups, Five FA Charity Shield Cups, four European Cups, one UEFA Cup and one UEFA Super Cup. He was capped 50 times for England.

Neal was a defender, who acquired the nickname Zico, the name of a Brazilian player, because of his ability to come forward and score important goals. In 650 games for the Reds he scored 59 goals and played 417 games consecutively. Neal took over as captain from Graeme Souness and was known for his skill and ability to read the game combined with "... an awareness of every other player in the side and what their job is", to quote Ray Clemence. Undoubtedly one of the greatest full-backs of his time, and a Liverpool legend, Phil Neal was said to have epitomised the spirit and passion at Liverpool.

He went on to manage a variety of teams after he left Liverpool in 1985.

31st March 1985. Division 1, Liverpool 0 v Manchester United 1, Phil Neal outjumps Manchester United's Jesper Olsen to win the high ball

ROSES ARE RED, THE FA CUP IS, TOO!

THE 1985/86 SEASON

Joe Fagan had stuck to his promise and handed over the reigns to an all-time Liverpool legend; Kenny Dalglish. After the Heysel tragedy, English clubs had been banned from European competitions, so it wasn't the best of times to take over. Nonetheless, Kenny proved that his talent was not restricted to the field of play and brought the Reds to the top of the division again. Player - manager Kenny also scored the winning goal against Chelsea at Stamford Bridge to win Liverpool the League Championship.

Liverpool reported back for duty this season with a wonderful double and a win they had been waiting for since 1974; the FA Cup. And they took it from …. yes! Everton! And it was a more than usually exciting league season, because the main rival turned out to be … Everton again, and it could have gone either way, as Liverpool only hit the top spot after the 36th game. But it didn't! Liverpool won every one of the last 7 games once they got to the top, treating fans to two electrified 5-0 goal feasts against Coventry and then Birmingham. They were undefeated in the final twelve games and walloped Oxford United 6-0.

One to forget that might have cost them the title was the game against … who else but Everton. Losing at home 2-0 when the Reds were fighting to get off third place was a setback, but the fight went on.

The League Cup was thrown away to middle-of-the-table QPR in the semi-final, 2-3 on aggregate, but the challenge for the one-off Super Cup, organised to compensate for the loss of European competitions, went like a bomb, and Liverpool took the semi-final honours from Norwich. As the final was played at the start of the 1986/87 season, I'll put the result there. It was a real humdinger for Liverpool, though, so don't worry! Against …

yes, you've guessed it!

10th May 1986. FA Cup Final, celebrating with the trophy

PLAYER DEBUTS

Two new boys this season. Midfielder Steve McMahon joined from Aston Villa and played on the 14th of September 1985. Mark Seagraves had come up through the youth system at Liverpool and he played in the League Cup semi-final against QPR on the twelfth of February 1986.

> 21st December 1985. Steve McMahon challenges Paul Gascoigne of Newcastle United

The fight for the top was ruthless and Everton were resurgent, so the Reds had double the motivation to take the honours. Manchester United came 4th and with the same number of points for the second season in a row.

This was the final table:

POS	TEAM	POINTS	GD
1	Liverpool	88	+52
2	Everton	86	+46
3	West Ham United	84	+34
4	Man. United	76	+34
5	Sheff. Wednesday	73	+09

West Ham held the Reds to a 1-1 draw in August 1985, but Everton had to take the blow of the 3-2 defeat at Goodison Park in September. Manchester United were held 1-1 at Old Trafford as were Sheffield Wednesday in January 1986 and Manchester United at Anfield in February. West Ham had fallen at Anfield 3-1 on January the 18th, but Everton got two in at Anfield to win 2-0. Sheffield took another draw in March at Bramall Lane in Sheffield, 0-0, to end the games against the top contenders for the league title.

> 14th September 1985. Alan Hansen beats Oxford United's John Aldridge in the air

THE STATISTICAL SEASON:

NUMBER OF GAMES:

Played	63
Won	41
Drawn	15
Lost	07

CLEAN SHEETS:

League	16
All Matches	24

GOALS SCORED:

League	89
All Matches	138

AVERAGE NUMBER OF GOALS SCORED IN EACH MATCH:

League	2.76
All Matches	2.72

AVERAGE NUMBER OF MINUTES REQUIRED FOR GOALS SCORED:

League	50
All Matches	52

AVERAGE HOME ATTENDANCE:

League	35,316
All Matches	31,592

CLASSIC MATCHES: 1985/86

LIVERPOOL V TOTTENHAM HOTSPUR, 4-1:

League Division One: Anfield, 28th September 1985

Liverpool were already heading upwards at this stage in the season and in this game they showed why. Nonetheless, for the first 40 minutes of the game, Ossie Ardiles and his London teammates played well and were on a par with the high-flying Liverpudlians. Liverpool were playing a hard game, as evidenced by the 3 minutes added on at the end of the first half, and the White Hart Lane boys allowed themselves to become rattled and there was a plethora of free kicks. Then Lawrenson struck just before the half-time whistle slotting one in from a narrow angle.

There followed a magnificent dive from Grobbelaar, only for Tottenham to draw level with a drive from Chiedozie that left Grobbelaar no chance. Oddly, Tottenham seemed to lose the plot after that and couldn't stop the flow of Liverpool goals. It took just ten minutes for Rush to get the next goal when a great Beglin pass found the striker, who hit from 15 yards out. Then it was two penalties that decided the match. The first may not have been justified, but the second certainly was when Rush was struck down. Mølby took them both and they whistled in for the final 4-1 score line.

1 Bruce Grobbelaar Goalkeeper
2 Phil Neal Defender
3 Jim Beglin Defender
4 Mark Lawrenson Defender
5 Ronnie Whelan Midfielder
6 Alan Hansen Defender
7 Kenny Dalglish Forward
8 Craig Johnston Midfielder
9 Ian Rush Forward
10 Jan Mølby Midfielder
11 Steve McMahon Midfielder
12 Kevin MacDonald Midfielder

LIVERPOOL V EVERTON 3-1:

FA Cup: Wembley, 10th May 1986

What can you do? It just so happens that Everton got clouted by the Reds in some very important games this season, so another classic has to be the FA Cup final game against the men in blue.

Liverpool were already League Champions, but hadn't won the FA Cup for 12 years. Yet Everton, it seemed, were going to get away with this one. Unusually, they had taken control of midfield from Liverpool, and that speedy lad Gary Lineker had been causing all manner of problems for Lawrenson in the Liverpool defence. The Liverpool forwards could make little headway at the other end either. So when Lineker put Everton ahead after 27 minutes, knocking it in after Grobbelaar had saved the initial shot, and almost saved the second, it was not looking good for the boys in red.

There were more close shaves in the second half, too, and no one expected Liverpool to survive except with a miracle. Especially as Dalglish wasn't on sparkling form and Grobbelaar had to stretch more than once to prevent a second goal for Everton.

Finally, Liverpool began to fire on all cylinders. It was maestro Rush who achieved the miracle and skillfully rounded the keeper to put the ball in for the equaliser on the 56th minute on the back of a deadly Liverpool attack. Whelan had almost been given the ball, and swift passing between him, Mølby – who played like a Trojan throughout and almost scored using some delightful ball play – and Rush led to the goal. A superb save from a Sharp header by Grobbelaar then rescued the Reds again.

Liverpool kept up the pressure and scissored through the Everton defence, and it was Rush and Mølby once more who were involved in the second goal when Rush went off down the left flank. Mølby took the pass and crossed the ball for Johnston to run clear and crack in the goal.

Everton sensed that they were losing the game and changed to all out attack leaving just three defenders. Liverpool attackers were now on the rampage and on 83 minutes came a superb, classic Liverpool goal. Rush was there again; he passed to Mølby, who swiftly sent the ball through to Whelan tearing down the middle. Whelan paused, saw Rush coming in, looped the ball perfectly to him and Rush drove the ball hard and low into the Everton net. There was no chance for the Everton team to come back. Liverpool had taken the FA Cup.

1 Bruce Grobbelaar Goalkeeper
2 Mark Lawrenson Defender
3 Jim Beglin Defender
4 Steve Nicol Midfielder
5 Ronnie Whelan Midfielder
6 Alan Hansen Defender
7 Kenny Dalglish Forward
8 Craig Johnston Midfielder
9 Ian Rush Forward
10 Jan Mølby Midfielder
11 Kevin MacDonald Midfielder
12 Steve McMahon Midfielder

10th May 1986. FA Cup Final, Ian Rush takes the ball around Everton goalkeeper Bobby Mimms

A CLASSIC MATCH MOMENT:

Liverpool v Everton 3-1
FA Cup: Wembley, 10th May 1986.

This one came when the cool-headed Whelan stopped momentarily in his swift run, saw Rush and looped a perfect ball to him that Rush drove hard and low into the net.

DERBY RESULTS:

TEAM	SCORE	TEAM	DATE
Everton	2-3	Liverpool	21st September 1985: Goodison
Liverpool	0-2	Everton	22nd February 1986: Anfield
Liverpool	3-1	Everton	10th May 1986: Wembley

PLAYER PROFILE: RONNIE WHELAN

Ronnie Whelan was born on the 25th September 1961 in Dublin, the Republic of Ireland, into a football family; his father played for the Republic of Ireland national team. Ronnie made his debut for Liverpool on the 3rd of April 1981 and made a total of 493 appearances in red, scoring 73 goals. He was also a Republic of Ireland international playing 53 times for his country. When Hansen was injured, Whelan took over as captain. Whelan was a skilled and hard-working midfielder, whose presence was vital to the winning Liverpool side of the 80s. Paisley called him "…our man for the big occasion". Whelan could score vital goals, and his reading of the game and the position of his teammates was second to none. His later career was beset with injuries that caused him to miss many vital games and he finally bowed out on the 7th of July 1994.

Whelan then joined Southend United as player-manager. He is now a TV pundit and after-dinner speaker. He is also a fundraiser and patron of a charity.

MANAGER PROFILE: KENNY DALGLISH

Born on the 4th March 1951 in Glasgow, Scotland, Kenny's first game in charge of Liverpool was played on the 17th August 1985 when the Reds beat Arsenal 2-0.

Having agreed to take over the manager position on the condition that Bob Paisley would stay at his side for two years, Dalglish became the first player-manager in the English game. He changed the team's style of play, and the team continued their winning ways beating Manchester United to the League title, and Everton in the FA Cup final.

King Kenny, as he was known amongst Liverpool supporters, managed the club during one of its most successful periods. In total as a player and manager he won the league First Division title, the FA Cup twice, the League Cup four times, three European Cups and the UEFA Super Cup.

In 1983 he won the Ballon d'Or Silver Award as well as PFA Player of the Year. He received the FWA Footballer of the Year in 1979 and 1983, and in 2009, Four Four Two named him as the greatest striker in post-war football in Britain. In 2006 he came top of the Liverpool fans' "100 Players Who Shook the Kop" poll and he has been inducted into both the English and Scottish Football Halls of Fame.

Dalglish went on to manage Blackburn Rovers, Newcastle United and Celtic before returning to Liverpool for one year in 2011 as caretaker manager. Liverpool won the League Cup that year.

IF YOU HAVE TEARS:

THE 1986/87 SEASON

It was ironic that in a season in which Rush scored 40 goals as top goalscorer, his second best tally, Liverpool once again failed to pick up any major honours. This was the second time in the silverware waterfall of the 80s that Liverpool found themselves in this position, the 84/85 season being the other. But Dalglish didn't want to spend rashly, and he had four players in mind that he wanted, and he was bravely prepared to wait to achieve his aims. It was a blow when Rush announced that he would be moving on to Juventus at the end of the season. Life was suddenly unpredictable at Anfield, and the 1-1 draw in the Charity Shield against Everton seemed to reflect that. The men in blue took the league title, with Liverpool 9 points behind on second place in a season of 11 losses when the longest unbeaten run was 5 games. In the English Super Cup final, however, Liverpool wiped their Merseyside rivals out completely, 7-2 on aggregate. Kevin MacDonald's leg was broken in two places, which was more or less the end of his career at Anfield, and the League Cup tie with Everton in January 1987 threw up an appalling incident that resulted in a shattered leg for Jim Beglin. It certainly was a difficult year all round.

The League Cup final was lost to Arsenal 1-2. This was the first time in 145 games when Ian Rush had scored that Liverpool had lost. The FA Cup challenge petered out in the third round after a second replay against Luton Town, which Liverpool lost 3-0.

The season of 'almost made it but not quite', was not devoid of highlights, though. There was a fabulous 6-2 drubbing of Norwich City and a 5-2 strike against West Ham United at Upton Park. Arsenal were beaten twice, perversely, and Everton once. Tottenham, too, got revenge for previous years and took two victories from their encounters with the Reds. But there was at least that goal record to delight in. Fulham came to Anfield in September 1986 and left totally desiccated, and deafened with the roaring in their ears that followed ten Liverpool goals. Five players raked the Fulham net in that goal feast extraordinaire! McMahon three times.

The Reds did challenge hard for the league title, however, and were on top spot after their 30th game against Luton Town. Then came the final 9 decisive games and they yielded just 3 wins, with three consecutive losses, 5 in total, which allowed Everton to slip past. There is more irony in the fact that the Reds played 6 games against Everton and were undefeated in all of them; two in the league, twice in the English Super Cup (7-2 to Liverpool on aggregate) and once in both the Charity Shield and the League Cup competition.

The season did mark a sea change at Liverpool, and it heralded the gradual passing of the unprecedented run of truly stunning performances that had raked in the honours up until then.

16th August 1986. Combined team photograph after the FA Charity Shield at Wembley

PLAYER DEBUTS

There were lots of new faces for the Kop to evaluate this season. Mike Hooper and Barry Venison both got their starts against Everton on the 16th of August 1986 in the Charity Shield. On the 7th of October it was John Durnin and Brian Mooney who got the chance to show what they could do against Fulham in the League Cup. In December up stepped Alan Irvine and Gary Ablett against Charlton Athletic. Then a name that would really please the Kop, John Aldridge, appeared on the 21st of February 1987 against Aston Villa. Last of the bunch was Nigel Spackman on the 25th of February 1987 in the Southampton game.

Oddly, in an otherwise disappointing season, Liverpool lost just three games against the top clubs in the league. Tottenham did the deed twice, 1-0 each time, and Norwich managed it at Carrow Road with a 2-1 win.

This was the final table:

POS	TEAM	POINTS	GD
1	Everton	86	+45
2	Liverpool	77	+33
3	Tott. Hotspur	71	+25
4	Arsenal	70	+23
5	Norwich City	68	+02

Arsenal were the first to meet Liverpool and went home with a 2-1 defeat to chew on. Another London club, Tottenham, had more luck in October with a 0-1 win at Anfield. A 6-2 thumping of Norwich then lifted hearts at Liverpool before a 1-1 draw against Everton in November at Goodison Park. Arsenal went down again in North London, 1-0 in March, and Tottenham repeated their act of destruction at White Hart Lane, also in March 1987, 1-0 again. That was closely followed by defeat at Norwich 1-2 and a final wallop around those blue ears at Anfield, where Everton went down 3-1.

22nd March 1987. Nigel Spackman in action against Tottenham Hotspur

THE STATISTICAL SEASON:

NUMBER OF GAMES:

Played	57
Won	31
Drawn	13
Lost	13

CLEAN SHEETS:

League	17
All Matches	24

GOALS SCORED:

League	72
All Matches	105

AVERAGE NUMBER OF GOALS SCORED IN EACH MATCH:

League	2.05
All Matches	2.44

AVERAGE NUMBER OF MINUTES REQUIRED FOR GOALS SCORED:

League	52
All Matches	50

AVERAGE HOME ATTENDANCE:

League	35,188
All Matches	33,586

CLASSIC MATCHES: 1986/87

LIVERPOOL V FULHAM 10-0:
League Cup: Anfield, 23rd September 1986

This one had to be mentioned simply because of the score line, a touch of history, witnessed by a mere 14,000 fans, as it was the biggest ever win for Liverpool in a League Cup game. Even though McMahon missed a penalty.

The fun started after just 8 minutes when Rush scored his first. The goals then mounted at regular intervals throughout; Wark, it was his first game of the season, on 10 minutes, Whelan on 28 minutes, McMahon on 44 minutes, Wark again on 63 minutes, McMahon again on 66 and his hat trick on 71 minutes. At that point Rush got back into the act and scored his second on 76 minutes before McMahon scored his 4th on 79 minutes. Nicol finished off the scoring on the 83rd minute. It was certainly McMahon's night; he was commanding in midfield. Rush failed to score at least another two when he hit the post, and his team mates failed to capitalise on their chances as the Reds washed over the Fulham defenders and dominated the game with a masterclass in precision passing and speed off the ball.

1 Bruce Grobbelaar Goalkeeper
2 Gary Gillespie Defender
3 Jim Beglin Defender
4 Mark Lawrenson Defender
5 Ronnie Whelan Midfielder
6 Alan Hansen Defender
7 Kenny Dalglish Forward
8 Steve Nicol Midfielder
9 Ian Rush Forward
10 John Wark Midfielder
11 Steve McMahon Midfielder
12 Mike Hooper Goalkeeper
13 Barry Venison Defender

EVERTON V LIVERPOOL 1-4:
English Super Cup: Goodison Park, 30th September 1986

Well, of course, this one deserved an honourable mention, at least. Another hat trick for Rush coming after a superb Mølby pass that gave him his third. His first, that a dive from Everton keeper Mimm could do nothing to stop, came after just 10 minutes, and his second was grace of another precision pass by Mølby that had him racing past the Everton offside trap. Everton were very unlucky with a shot deflected onto the bar and a missed penalty. But Nicol volleyed his goal on the 62nd minute and it was as good as over for Everton, now 4 in arrears. Sharp hit one for Everton on 88 minutes, but that was all the blue rivals could manage with their under-performing team. 7-2 to Liverpool on aggregate. Very satisfying indeed.

1 Bruce Grobbelaar Goalkeeper
2 Gary Gillespie Defender
3 Jim Beglin Defender
4 Mark Lawrenson Defender
5 Ronnie Whelan Midfielder
6 Alan Hansen Defender
7 John Wark Midfielder
8 Steve Nicol Midfielder
9 Ian Rush Forward
10 Jan Mølby Midfielder
11 Steve McMahon Midfielder
12 Barry Venison Defender
13 Paul Walsh Forward

22nd March 1987. Tottenham defender Richard Gough takes a ride on the back of Liverpool's Ian Rush

WIMBLEDON V LIVERPOOL, 1-3:

League Division One: Plough Lane, 4th October 1986

Only one of 8 games that Liverpool won away this season. Wimbledon began well, playing to their strength, which was the high ball for the tall men up front, John Fashanu especially, who almost scored, as did Sanchez. This situation was dangerous for Liverpool for the first 15 minutes of the game when it was vital to keep the headers away from the goal. But the threat was brought under control, and Liverpool began the dissection of the defence, an art for which they were renowned. They missed a clutch of opportunities and only began to get going when Jan Mølby opened the scoring on the 50th minute after some lovely interplay with McMahon. Mølby was given enough time to contemplate his low shot, so he calmly chose his spot. At that point, Rush decided it was his turn and scored 6 minutes later after more ball play between Whelan, McMahon and himself. McMahon sped forward with the ball, put a pacy through-ball in Rush's path and Rush drove it home across the keeper, with his right foot.

To their credit, Wimbledon never gave up and slapped in a goal on 82 minutes after Grobbelaar had deflected a shot from Wise and a lobbed ball, returned to the far side of the goal, saw Fairweather sail up to meet it and nod it into the net.

Jan Mølby helped Rush to his second on the 90th minute with a long through ball that Rush coolly headed past the Wimbledon keeper, way off his line because the defence had been caught napping, and the Liverpool striker then simply stroked the ball into the open goal.

1 **Bruce Grobbelaar** Goalkeeper
2 **Gary Gillespie** Defender
3 **Jim Beglin** Defender
4 **Mark Lawrenson** Defender
5 **Ronnie Whelan** Midfielder
6 **Alan Hansen** Defender
7 **John Wark** Midfielder
8 **Steve Nicol** Midfielder
9 **Ian Rush** Forward
10 **Jan Mølby** Midfielder
11 **Steve McMahon** Midfielder
12 **Barry Venison** Defender

25th April 1987. Jan Molby in control against Everton

A CLASSIC MATCH MOMENT:

Wimbledon v Liverpool, 1-3
League Division One: Plough Lane, 4th October 1986.

Truly classic Liverpool this one, when McMahon took off with the ball, sent a beautiful through-ball into the path of Rush charging forward in support. Rush right-footed the ball across the keeper and into the net.

DERBY RESULTS:

TEAM	SCORE	TEAM	DATE
Liverpool	0-0	Everton	16th August 1986: Wembley: Charity Shield
Liverpool	3-1	Everton	16th September 1986: Anfield: English Super Cup
Everton	1-4	Liverpool	30th September 1986: Goodison Park: English Super Cup
Everton	0-0	Liverpool	23rd November 1986: Goodison Park
Everton	0-1	Liverpool	21st January 1987: Goodison Park: League Cup, R5Park: English Super Cup
Liverpool	3-1	Everton	25th April 1987: Anfield: English Super Cup

PLAYER PROFILE:

BRUCE GROBBELAAR ▼

Born on October the 6th 1957 in Durban, Union of South Africa, Grobbelaar was raised in Zimbabwe and after coming to Liverpool's attention when he was with Crewe Alexandra, he joined Liverpool in 1981. He stayed with the northern side until February 1994, by which time he had made 628 appearances for them. Often criticised and at the same time loved for his antics on the field, Grobbelaar was a keeper of the highest rank, who often pulled off spectacular saves, although it took him some time to eradicate the errors in his game when he first joined the club. However, Grobbelaar gave short shrift to his own mistakes and those of his team mates; it was not unknown for him to react with fury at defensive misunderstandings.

Nonetheless, with the approval of Bob Paisley, Grobbelaar's antics were in full cry during the penalty shootout against A.S. Roma in 1984 and were rewarded with two missed attempts by the Italians.

When he left Liverpool, Grobbelaar went to Southampton and a variety of other clubs. He now lives in Canada and is still active in the football world.

29th April 1987. Bruce Grobbelaar lies injured as trainer Roy Evans and referee B. Stevens assist

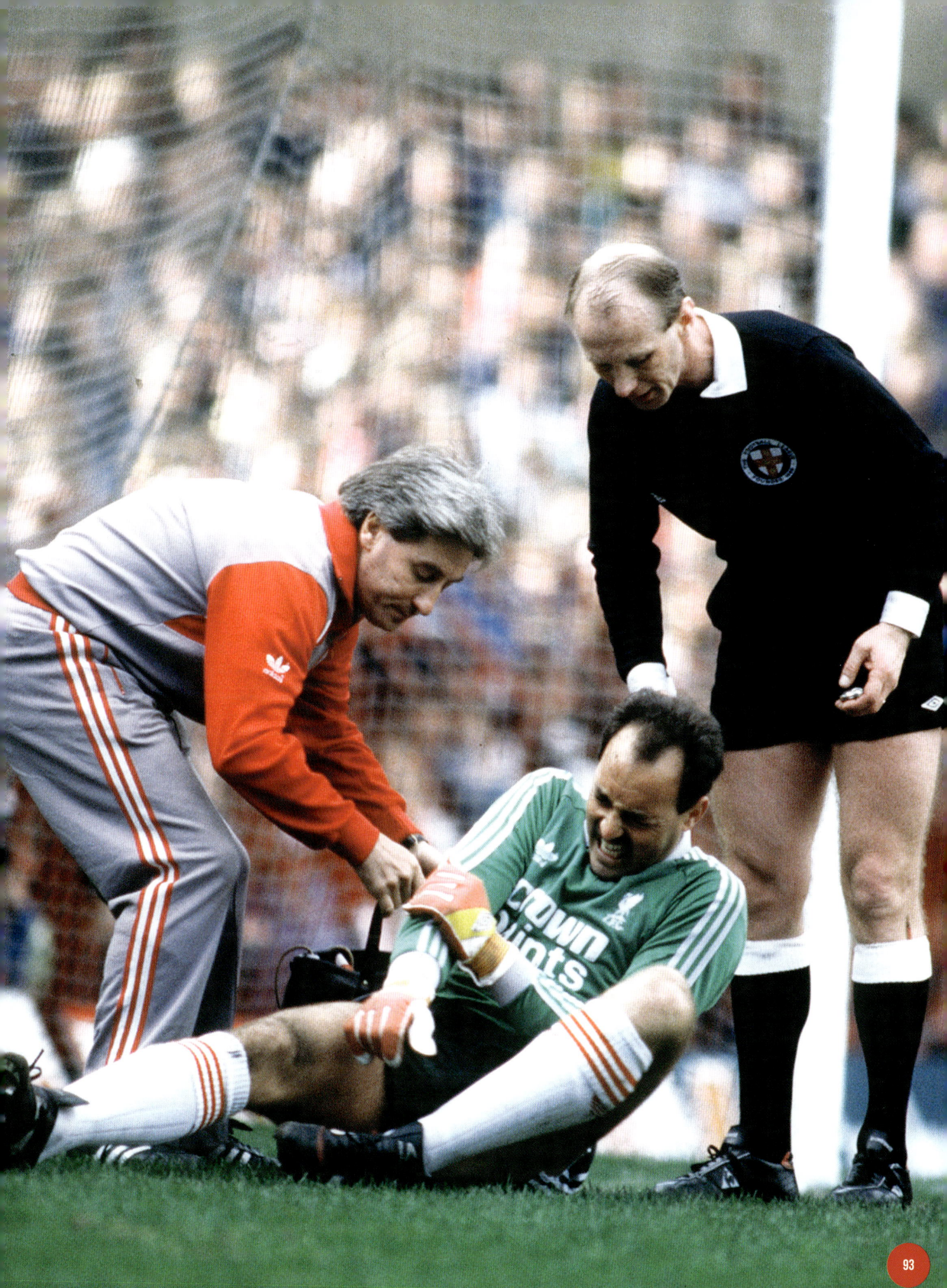

MASTERS OF THE LEAGUE:
THE 1987/88 SEASON

It wasn't as spectacular in terms of trophies gained as some that had gone before and there was 'just' the league title to show for the season's efforts, their 17th league title. But what a league season it was, nonetheless! Was this the greatest team ever, not only in Liverpool but in England? Such questions showed just how good this squad was. Only two league games were lost; against Everton away, 1-0, and Nottingham Forest away, 1-2. But for a host of drawn games, 12 in all, the 90 points at the end could easily have been 115, especially if the home games had been won. The statistics are still impressive. Four games in a row won with 4 goals on the Liverpool scorecard; three of those with clean sheets. 9 games where 4 goals were scored, 10 games with just one goal scored against them, and 29 games without defeat, equalling a Football League record. John Aldridge scored in 9 consecutive games and became top goalscorer with 29 goals, and there was a spectacular 5-0 dismembering of Nottingham Forest that was described as the "… finest exhibition I've seen", by Sir Tom Finney. QPR, Arsenal, Newcastle United, Coventry and Sheffield Wednesday were just some of the teams beaten home and away. Liverpool romped home in the league, 9 points clear of Manchester United. Everton were out of sight on 70.

Oddly, for a team playing such high quality football, they lost 1-0 to Wimbledon in the FA Cup final and fell to Everton in round three of the League Cup having struggled to subdue Blackburn Rovers. Someone by the name of John Barnes was voted Player of the Year by the Football Writer's Association and the PFA.

15 August 1987. John Aldridge celebrates after scoring against Arsenal

PLAYER DEBUTS

Again there were several new faces for the Kop to cheer this season. Liverpool crowds would feel the thrill from witnessing one of the greatest players in English football, who arrived to play against Arsenal on the 15th of August 1987; John Barnes. Peter Beardsley played in the same match for his first time in red. This was the year that Ray Houghton started against Luton Town on the 24th of October, and on the 5th of March 1988, Alex Watson took part in his first game.

▲ 4th April 1988. United's Brian McClair is beaten by Peter Beardsley

Liverpool had a wonderful league season in which they were defeated just twice, both times against top clubs in the league. Nottingham Forest were winners at home and Everton got away with a 1-0 win at Goodison Park.

This was the final table:

POS	TEAM	POINTS	GD
1	Liverpool	90	+63
2	Man. United	81	+33
3	Nott. Forest	73	+28
4	Everton	70	+26
5	QPR`	67	+10

QPR were the first to feel the sting this season with a 4-0 drubbing at Anfield where Everton also took a kicking, going down 2-0 just two weeks later. Manchester United were held to a 1-1 draw at Old Trafford, and in March 1988, QPR lost again, 1-0, at Loftus Road. Everton were luckier and won 1-0 at Goodison Park, a defeat followed shortly after by another against Nottingham Forest at the City Ground, 2-1; and Manchester stole another draw, 2-2 at Anfield in April 1988. Forest were walloped at Anfield later in April, 5-0, the last of the matches against the top contenders for the league title.

August 1987. John Barnes performs an overhead kick above David O'Leary of Arsenal ▲

THE STATISTICAL SEASON:

NUMBER OF GAMES:
Played	50
Won	32
Drawn	14
Lost	04

CLEAN SHEETS:
League	21
All Matches	27

GOALS SCORED:
League	87
All Matches	99

AVERAGE NUMBER OF GOALS SCORED IN EACH MATCH:
League	2.45
All Matches	2.22

AVERAGE NUMBER OF MINUTES REQUIRED FOR GOALS SCORED:
League	53
All Matches	53

AVERAGE HOME ATTENDANCE:
League	39,682
All Matches	39,429

CLASSIC MATCHES: 1987/88

NEWCASTLE UNITED V LIVERPOOL 1-4:
League Division One: St. James's Park, 20th September 1987

Liverpool's performance in this match was described as 'majestic'. It was Nicol and Aldridge who shone that day in a side that displayed its ability to move forward with devastating speed and coupled that with individual excellence. Liverpool had an iron grip on this game throughout as the forwards tore into the Newcastle defence, whilst their own defenders had the luxury of being able to move well up in support of the attacks that swirled over the grass.

For Peter Beardsley, it was a chance to show his former club what they were missing, and what better way than to be involved in the build up for the first goal.

It truly was Nicol's hour of glory, though, because he popped in a hat trick. Yet it still took Liverpool 20 minutes to get into their stride and the ball in the net. There had been little in the way of goalmouth action until John Barnes and Beardsley combined their efforts and brought Liverpool the lead. Barnes adeptly fought his way past three Newcastle men, passed to Beardsley, took the return ball, his cross went to Nicol by way of Anderson. Nicol struck, and Liverpool were one up.

The second was in after 38 minutes and again involved Barnes who, under pressure, caught a looping cross from Venison and nodded the ball down perfectly to Aldridge, who hooked a right-footed shot into the net. 6 goals in six outings for the striker.

Beardsley almost scored, too, and with another Nicol goal disallowed for offside, the third had to wait until three minutes into the second half. Beardsley streaked down the flank, split the Newcastle defence wide open to pick up a long pass and, ever generous to his teammates and rubbing salt into Newcastle's wounds, passed a perfect ball through a gap to Nicol, who put the Reds three ahead. Nicol admitted later that he, in fact, mishit the strike. No matter, in it went.

With Liverpool in command in midfield, Newcastle were given a penalty on the 61st minute after Gillespie was ruled to have taken down Mirandinha – whose ball control was always a cause for concern in the Liverpool ranks – after he had broken through into the Liverpool penalty area. McDonald put the spot kick away for the St. James side. That started an energetic fight back from Newcastle. Mirandinha was a menace anywhere near the goal.

But the fun wasn't over yet for the fans in red and Liverpool contained the resurgent opposition as they set about getting the next goal. This was Nicol's third after Aldridge swivelled with the ball to put his teammate though. Aldridge latched onto the pass and took off at high speed to confront the Newcastle keeper, at which point he chipped the ball over the keeper's head and into the net. Later, Nicol would, understandably, mark this game down as a very special one for him..

1 **Bruce Grobbelaar** Goalkeeper
2 **Gary Gillespie** Defender
3 **Barry Venison** Defender
4 **Steve Nicol** Midfielder
5 **Ronnie Whelan** Midfielder
6 **Alan Hansen** Defender
7 **Peter Beardsley** Forw/Midf

8 **John Aldridge** Striker
9 **Mark Lawrenson** Defender
10 **John Barnes** Winger
11 **Steve McMahon** Midfielder
12 **Nigel Spackmann** Midfielder
13 **Paul Walsh** Forward

LIVERPOOL V NOTTINGHAM FOREST 5-0:
League Division One: Anfield, 13th April 1988

An unforgettable football display that must be one of the top Liverpool performances of all time. Described in The Times as "… as breathtaking, as enchanting and as riveting as the most lavish firework display", the game showed the Liverpool players firing on all cylinders, with Barnes and Beardsley tormenting the Forest

20th September 1987. John Barnes evades Newcastle United's Glyn Hodges and David McCreery

defence. Forest were no match for Liverpool's speed, accuracy and inventive play, and just after the 18-minute mark, the dam broke when Ray Houghton surged into the defenders and kept running as he passed to Barnes, whose quick return was taken past the defence by Houghton and slotted in beside Forest keeper Sutton.

Then Aldridge sprinted forward onto a 30-yard Beardsley pass that knifed through the Forest defence. Aldridge looped the ball over the keeper for number two after 37 minutes.

Forest keeper Sutton had his work cut out, and it was only his myriad of astounding reactions that saved a complete rout.

Beardsley had a terrific match and was almost rewarded with a goal when his shot hit the bar after he had outmaneuvered a whole segment of the Forest defence. It was Houghton who delivered the pass to Gary Gillespie that enabled him to hammer in a volley almost on the hour. Then it was Beardsley himself who picked up the next goal on 79 minutes. Barnes had outsmarted two Forest men and sent the ball on to Beardsley, whose drive flew into the net.

It was left to Aldridge to put in number 5, four minutes from the end. Spackman showed his skills, taking the ball, running forward and passing to Aldridge in front of goal, who was clear for his second two minutes from time.

1 **Bruce Grobbelaar** Goalkeeper
2 **Gary Gillespie** Defender
3 **Gary Ablett** Defender
4 **Steve Nicol** Midfielder
5 **Nigel Spackman** Midfielder
6 **Alan Hansen** Defender
7 **Peter Beardsley** Midfielder
8 **John Aldridge** Striker
9 **Ray Houghton** Midfielder
10 **John Barnes** Winger
11 **Steve McMahon** Midfielder
12 **Craig Johnston** Forward
13 **Jan Mølby** Midfielder

LIVERPOOL V ARSENAL 2-0:
League Division One: Anfield, 16th January 1988

Liverpool made the first quarter of an hour their own, but Arsenal got back into the game and the defence became impenetrable. It was only on the 44th minute that Aldridge was sent the ball that he struck for Liverpool's first goal. Barnes, who showed his brilliance throughout, had seared through the Arsenal men, and when McMahon kept the ball in play, he, too, scythed through the Arsenal defence and slipped the ball on to Beardsley. He had surged onwards to set up an unmarked Aldridge in front of goal. A superb display of Liverpool teamwork.

It was Beardsley, as slippery as an eel, who struck a tremendous goal on the 61st minute. Again, precision passing, from Spackman this time, and swift interplay from Aldridge released Beardsley, who worked his way past the defence and into the penalty area for a clear shot at goal, and he chipped the ball in over the keeper. A superb goal. "Pure genius", as the TV pundits said when they saw it.

1 **Mike Hooper** Goalkeeper
2 **Gary Gillespie** Defender
3 **Mark Lawrenson** Defender
4 **Steve Nicol** Midfielder
5 **Ronnie Whelan** Midfielder
6 **Alan Hansen** Defender
7 **Peter Beardsley** Midfielder
8 **John Aldridge** Striker
9 **Ray Houghton** Midfielder
10 **John Barnes** Winger
11 **Steve McMahon** Midfielder
12 **Craig Johnston** Forward
14 **Nigel Spackman** Midfielder

13th April 1988. Bruce Grobbelaar jokes with the fans behind his goal

A CLASSIC MATCH MOMENT:

Liverpool v Arsenal 2-0

League Division One: Anfield, 16th January 1988

Hardworking Beardsley caused the Arsenal defence all manner of problems until he finally jinked and jogged his way in front of goal after precision passing from Spackman and fast reactions from Aldridge. Beardsley chipped the ball in over the keeper. Wonderful football.

DERBY RESULTS:

TEAM	SCORE	TEAM	DATE
Liverpool	0-1	Everton	28th October 1987: Anfield: League Cup, R3
Liverpool	2-0	Everton	1st November 1987: Anfield
Everton	0-1	Liverpool	21st February 1988: Goodison Park: FA cup R5
Everton	1-0	Liverpool	20th March 1988: Goodison Park

PLAYER PROFILE:

JOHN ALDRIDGE

Born in Garston, Liverpool on the 18th September 1958, he made his Liverpool debut on the 21st of February 1987 and appeared for the Reds on 104 occasions until September 1989, scoring 63 goals. He scored in each of the first nine games of the 1987/88 season. He was a master at reading the positioning of his teammates and channelling the ball to them, then hovering in front of goal and lethal at finishing. He was leading goalscorer that season with 29 goals. His total as a player over his career amounted to 476, an astonishing tally. With Barnes and Beardsley he was part of one of the most thrilling attacking trios in Liverpool history. Having taken over from Ian Rush, he then found himself having to compete with him when Rush returned from Juventus and was given priority on the field. Aldridge left in 1989 to go to Real Sociedad.

Aldridge later went to Tranmere Rovers and became their manager. He also played for the Republic of Ireland 69 times.

Since retiring, Aldridge has become involved in providing football commentary on radio and TV.

9th April 1998. John Aldridge is lifted into the air by adoring fans

THE BLUES SEE RED

THE 1988/89 SEASON

As the decade of outstanding success began to draw to a close, there were two trophies for Liverpool; the Charity Shield, when Wimbledon were beaten 2-1, and the FA Cup, won in a nail-biting match against Everton – for the second time in that decade – 3-2. The League Championship title was lost after a spellbinding race to the top with Arsenal, in the closest finish ever in league football. Liverpool lost the title on goal difference after Arsenal scored in the last minute of the season. That's how it goes.

Mark Lawrenson had retired, but Ian Rush had returned unexpectedly to join a team that now boasted Rush, Aldridge, Barnes and Beardsley in its ranks. This was the season when the appalling disaster at Hillsborough before the start of the FA Cup semi-final against Nottingham Forest at Sheffield Wednesday on April the 15th 1989 would overshadow everything. Police had opened the gates hoping to ease congestion in the streets. The resultant crush cost 96 Liverpool supporters their lives.

Steve Nicol was voted the Football Writers' Association Player of the Year. John Aldridge was top goalscorer for the second year in a row; his tally was 31 goals. An 18-game undefeated run was brought to a screeching end by Arsenal at Anfield in the final match of the season. Losing to bottom of the table Newcastle 1-2 at home threw away the title as did losing to Norwich City at home. For a team of the quality of the Reds, Liverpool bounced around the table a lot and only hit the top for the first time in April 1989. But there were two goal feasts when Luton were flattened 5-0 and West Ham 5-1. Middlesborough did little better and were battered 3-0 and 4-0.

Second in the league, then, but an FA Cup to shout about. Most teams would have been more than pleased; but for a Liverpool side used to more trophy success in a season there were regrets, of course.

29th August 1988. Mercantile Credit Football League Centenary Trophy match

PLAYER DEBUTS

Three new boys this season; defender Steve Staunton was the first to get his chance against Tottenham on the 17th of September 1988. He stayed at the club until 2000, although he only made 148 appearances. He was closely followed by David Burrows, whose last of 193 appearances came in 1993. He ran out for the first time against Coventry City on the 22nd of October 1988. Finally, it was Mike Marsh's turn on the 1st of March 1989 against Charlton Athletic. Marsh also departed in 1993 after 101 games in red.

26th May 1989. Steve Staunton and Ronnie Whelan hold off Arsenal's Kevin Richardson

Liverpool drew against just one club in the top five; Arsenal. Everton were not in contention this season and came in on 8th place, and neither were Manchester United who were 11th. Tottenham did better but were just outside of the top five. Liverpool only won 4 of the games against the top clubs in the league. Nottingham Forest, Norwich City and twice against Derby County.

This was the final table:

POS	TEAM	POINTS	GD
1	Arsenal	76	+37
2	Liverpool	76	+37
3	Nott. Forest	64	+21
4	Norwich City	62	+03
5	Derby County	58	+02

Nottingham Forest showed that Liverpool were struggling a little when they took the points, 2-1, in October 1988. The Reds managed a draw at Arsenal 1-1 in December but lost to Norwich at Anfield the following week. Another week on and Derby County were taken down at the Baseball Ground 1-0 and again in March 1989 at Anfield, also 1-0. Norwich then lost 1-0 at Carrow Road as did Nottingham Forest, who came to Anfield and fell to a single goal. Then that final fateful match against Arsenal at home and the 2-0 loss that gave Arsenal the league title.

28th May 1989. John Barnes celebrates the winning goal with Ian Rush

THE STATISTICAL SEASON:

NUMBER OF GAMES:	
Played	53
Won	33
Drawn	12
Lost	08

CLEAN SHEETS:	
League	17
All Matches	22

GOALS SCORED:	
League	65
All Matches	98

AVERAGE NUMBER OF GOALS SCORED IN EACH MATCH:	
League	1.74
All Matches	1.87

AVERAGE NUMBER OF MINUTES REQUIRED FOR GOALS SCORED:	
League	52
All Matches	54

AVERAGE HOME ATTENDANCE:	
League	38,700
All Matches	36,863

CLASSIC MATCHES: 1988/89

LIVERPOOL V NOTTINGHAM FOREST 3-1:

FA Cup semi-final: Old Trafford; 7th May 1989

This was the replay of the match that had been abandoned after the Hillsborough tragedy. Liverpool wanted to win this one for all their fans who had lost their lives that day, because that would make it a Merseyside cup final. And they made their supporters proud with the performance they gave.

This, said the newspapers, was Liverpool at their phenomenal best, tackling as though they would bring down houses, fighting as though this was the last game they would ever play. None fought harder than McMahon, who would have stopped the devil that day.

The first goal waited just four minutes before it burst the game open, when a long-range Ray Houghton cross, sailed towards Barnes. It would never have reached him if two defenders hadn't got into a muddle and fallen over one another. Barnes, surprised but grateful, hammered a fierce shot at goal forcing a magnificent save from keeper Sutton. But Aldridge was lurking, and the rebound looped out to him. He reacted like lightning and headed the ball with just the right amount of power over Sutton for the first goal.

Having been almost without goal chances until then, Forest surprisingly drew level on 33 minutes. A tricky ball in the Liverpool defence led to a Hansen clearance that fell to Clough. Webb hammered Clough's pass towards the goal. The ball bounced, which led to Grobbelaar not catching it cleanly and it went over the line.

Aldridge almost got one after Barnes had displayed his unique ball skills yet again to beat a clutch of defenders and crossed the ball. Aldridge hit the woodwork.

Liverpool had to wait until the second half to strike again. It was another superb Liverpool lesson in teamwork. A short corner saw Houghton and Barnes unite to slice the defence and give Houghton the chance to cross. Aldridge went up and headed home number 2 on the 58th minute.

The nail in Forest's coffin came in the 72nd minute. Liverpool were always dangerous but just couldn't make their attacks pay off. But with the Liverpool forwards swooping like hawks and with Beardsley at his back, the ball jumped just as Laws went for it, after incisive Liverpool passing, and Laws stabbed the ball into his own goal for number three.

It was an emotional game on and off the pitch. Tears flowed freely and painful memories were still fresh. But the result was the right one.

1 **Bruce Grobbelaar** Goalkeeper
2 **Gary Ablett** Defender
3 **Steve Staunton** Defender
4 **Steve Nicol** Midfielder
5 **Ronnie Whelan** Midfielder
6 **Alan Hansen** Defender
7 **Peter Beardsley** Midfielder
8 **John Aldridge** Striker
9 **Ray Houghton** Midfielder
10 **John Barnes** Winger
11 **Steve McMahon** Midfielder
12 **Barry Venison** Defender
14 **Ian Rush** Forward

1989. John Aldridge celebrates as he scores a goal during the FA Cup Semi Final against Nottingham Forest

LIVERPOOL V EVERTON, 3-2:
FA Cup Final: Wembley; 25th May 1989

This Merseyside final was to be a memorial in memory of the Hillsborough fans. The semi against Forest had been important, but now that they were in the final and it was a derby match, Liverpool were resolute to a man that this game would not escape them. They felt that they owed a victory to their fans and those who were grieving. For Dalglish, the game was the to be the "greatest moment" of his career.

It was a match to savour. Liverpool, as they had so often, lay down the rules from the start with a goal that was as thrilling as it was swift in coming. It took four minutes for Aldridge to strike. Nicol found McMahon with one of those immaculate, long Liverpool passes, and he sent Aldridge charging through. Keeper Southall could only watch as the ball passed him.

From then until the 89th minute when Stuart McCall equalised with a last gasp goal, Liverpool dominated the midfield with Whelan and McMahon in a game that was described as the "... finest and most dramatic in memory". Barnes was dazzling and as dangerous as a razor blade. Liverpool continually outmatched Everton with some scintillating displays of skill and speed. And should have sewn the game up well before the final whistle, with Aldridge and Beardsley and Barnes coming so close. Only as the game began to approach the end did Everton put real pressure on the Liverpool defence.

Dalglish made a brave and probably match-winning decision. It changed the game and, perhaps, Aldridge's career when he was taken off and Ian Rush substituted on the 72nd minute. Perhaps he should have substituted the exhausted Staunton much earlier than the 91st minute; the Reds might have been spared extra time because the youngster was flailing against Nevin and Nevin was instrumental when McCall got the equaliser on 89 minutes after Grobbelaar failed to hold a low cross

The real thrills began in extra time. Rush repaid Dalglish's confidence in him by showing his old ability in spades and cracking home a superb second Liverpool goal in the 94th minute. Nicol saw the opportunity and played in a stunning ball to Rush in the penalty area. Rush guarded it like a jewel, turned, with the defender Ratcliffe behind him, and drove the ball into the net as he spun around. It was a special goal.

Everton were rewarded with a looping goal by McCall again, on 102 minutes after Hansen had headed the ball into his path, and that brought the Blues back into the match; but only for a minute, because Rush hit back and scored the winner on the 103rd minute rocking the Blues back on their heels. Whelan, McMahon and Barnes had begun the move across the field. Barnes spotted Rush and instantly sent over a pinpoint cross. Rush went hurtling in, cleverly and bravely headed the ball down and under the keeper for the winning goal.

A last ditch Everton attempt from a free kick whistled over the Liverpool goal and Liverpool had won the FA Cup for the second time in the 80s.

1 Bruce Grobbelaar Goalkeeper
2 Gary Ablett Defender
3 Steve Staunton Defender
4 Steve Nicol Midfielder
5 Ronnie Whelan Midfielder
6 Alan Hansen Defender
7 Peter Beardsley Midfielder
8 John Aldridge Striker
9 Ray Houghton Midfielder
10 John Barnes Winger
11 Steve McMahon Midfielder
12 Barry Venison Defender
14 Ian Rush Forward

25th May 1989. Kevin Ratcliffe of Everton brings down John Barnes

A CLASSIC MATCH MOMENT:

Liverpool v Everton 3-2
FA Cup Final: Wembley; 25th May 1989

Rush's final goal was Liverpool at their decisive best. Barnes sent over a superb cross, Rush went hurtling in and ingeniously headed the ball down and under the keeper for the winning goal.

DERBY RESULTS:

TEAM	SCORE	TEAM	DATE
Liverpool	1-1	Everton	11th December 1988: Anfield
Everton	0-0	Liverpool	3rd May 1989: Goodison Park
Liverpool	3-2	Everton	20th May 1989: Wembley

PLAYER PROFILE:
JOHN BARNES ▼

Born on the 7th of November 1963 in Kingston, Jamaica, he made his Liverpool debut on the 15th of August 1987 against Arsenal. He scored his first goal against Oxford United on the 12th of September when Liverpool won 2-1. In ten years at the club he made 407 appearances for Liverpool scoring 108 goals and was regarded as one of his club's and the country's best players. With Liverpool he won the Football League First Division twice, the FA Cup twice, and the League Cup and Charity Shield once. He was a member of the team that won the Football League First Division PFA Team of the Year three times, was voted PFA Players Player of the Year in 1988 and was voted FWA Footballer of the Year in 1988 and 1990. In 1990 he scored a personal best of 22 league goals beating Ian Rush. He became an MBE in 1998 and was inducted into the English Football Hall of Fame in 2005. On the 6th September 1995, Barnes won his 79th and last international cap for England.

Barnes was an extremely talented and graceful player, who delivered exciting, fast-moving football and scored 198 goals over his career. For many he was possibly the best player in the world at the end of the 80s and FourFourTwo magazine declared him to be the best Liverpool player ever.

Barnes married twice and had two sons and two daughters with his first wife Suzy and two daughters with Andrea his second wife. Barnes became a football manager, and after he retired from the game, was also a successful singer as well as a TV pundit

ONE MORE FOR THE ROAD

THE 1989/90 SEASON

The final season in this decade-long, high-adrenalin ride for Liverpool ended appropriately with another league title, the 18th. Sadly, it ushered in an era in which Liverpool would never again reach the same giddy heights, and a league title was not amongst the trophies gathered in the following decades.

Ian Rush was on good form with 26 goals, but John Barnes was top goalscorer with 28 that season. Jim Beglin had moved on, and John Aldridge, the only man to have scored a hat trick in three successive seasons during the glorious 80s, knew that he had lost his place to Ian Rush and left in September 1989 for Real Sociedad in Spain.

The season started well, with a 1-0 win over Arsenal in the Charity Shield in August, a small thrill of revenge for the events in the final game of the previous season. The league brought two victories against Everton – there were just two derby games this season and Liverpool emerged as victors in both – and also Chelsea – one of which was a 5-2 win at Stamford Bridge – and six other clubs besides. It brought double draws against Aston Villa, Nottingham forest, Norwich City and Luton Town. The most entertaining results came when poor Crystal Palace were absolutely taken to pieces, 9-1 at Anfield, and Coventry were decimated 6-1 at Highfield Road in the last game of the season.

All in all, five games were lost, and Liverpool sat atop the division for most of the time; the worst defeat came at Southampton, 1-4.

Crystal Palace had sweet revenge for their crushing defeats in the league; they beat Liverpool 3-4 in the FA Cup semi-final. Arsenal had their revenge, too, with a -1-0 victory in round three of the League Cup after Wigan had been slapped down, 8-2 on aggregate, in round two.

The Reds finally got a solid grip on the top spot after their 30th outing, against Southampton on the 31st of March 1990, which gave them a 3-2 win at home. The title was won on the 28th April against QPR in a 2-1 win at Anfield with two games left to play. By then, fans had seen Manchester United beaten at Old Trafford, 2-1, and exciting football that had yielded a host of goals, 107 in total; the Reds failed to score in just 7 games. And the terror of defenders, John Barnes, won the Player of the year award.

A mixed season, then, to end the glory years. Kenny Dalglish would be gone the following year and the Reds would have to wait until 2001 (they won the FA Cup, the League Cup and the UEFA Cup) to have similar success to the super-teams of the 80s that had set the fans' hearts on fire with pride and delight.

4th Nov 1989. John Barnes of Liverpool volleys the ball just wide against Coventry City

PLAYER DEBUTS

Swedish star player Glenn Hysén arrived to play for the first time against Arsenal on the 12th of August 1989 in the Charity Shield match. Later that year, on the 2nd of December, Nick Tanner lined up against Manchester City, and on the 31st of March 1990, it was the turn of Ronny Rosenthal to see what he could do against Southampton.

> 6th August 1989. Glenn Hysen takes on Luton Town's Roy Wegerle

Liverpool, the only representative for the north, lost just one game against a top club in this title-winning season when three London clubs made it into the top five; they lost to Tottenham Hotspur 1-0 at White Hart Lane. Otherwise there were four victories and three draws. Neither Everton, on 6th place, nor Manchester United, on 13th, made the grade this year.

This was the final table:

POS	TEAM	POINTS	GD
1	Liverpool	79	+41
2	Aston Villa	70	+19
3	Tott. Hotspur	63	+12
4	Arsenal	62	+16
5	Chelsea	60	+08

Aston Villa were the hard men this season, and Liverpool came away from Villa Park with a 1-1 draw in August 1989. The first win against the big boys had to wait until October and Tottenham, who were vanquished 1-0 at Anfield. In November, Arsenal were snuffed out again, 2-1 at Anfield, and Aston Villa took another draw from their game at Anfield in December. One week later, Chelsea got the first of their hidings, 5-2 at Stamford Bridge. In March 1990, Tottenham had better luck at White Hart Lane and won 1-0. That was the best result the London clubs could manage, because Arsenal could only get a draw from the Reds at Highbury, 1-1, and Chelsea crashed again, 4-1 at Anfield in April.

2nd December 1989. Peter Beardsley

THE STATISTICAL SEASON:

NUMBER OF GAMES:
Played	50
Won	30
Drawn	13
Lost	07

CLEAN SHEETS:
League	12
All Matches	19

GOALS SCORED:
League	78
All Matches	107

AVERAGE NUMBER OF GOALS SCORED IN EACH MATCH:
League	2.00
All Matches	2.44

AVERAGE NUMBER OF MINUTES REQUIRED FOR GOALS SCORED:
League	47
All Matches	49

AVERAGE HOME ATTENDANCE:
League	36,873
All Matches	34,814

CLASSIC MATCHES: 1989/90

LIVERPOOL V QPR, 2-1:
League Division One: Anfield; 28th April 1990

This was the one that saw Liverpool take the league title once again, for the tenth time in fifteen seasons. In fact they won the title by a handsome margin of 9 points.

The game began with what Liverpool fans had become used to, one way or another; an early goal by the opposition. QPR took the lead and with Liverpool unable to raise their game, they might have gone even further behind during the first half an hour, because QPR were playing well in midfield. A great shot even beat Grobbelaar but hit the bar. Added to that, the Liverpool defence was not at its best when free kicks or corners tested its resolve. It was a corner that did the initial damage when a ball from McDonald caused upset in the Liverpool area and Wegerle pushed the ball over the line.

During the last 15 minutes of the first half, Liverpool found their balance again and an equaliser looked on the cards. It eventually came after 40 minutes and some great teamwork between Nicol and Barnes. The cross then found Rush at the far post, and the lethal forward took his chance for a great goal. Under pressure from the QPR defence, he nonetheless calmly controlled the ball, and as it rose from a bounce, he hammered it in with uncanny accuracy from a very narrow angle.

A penalty awarded after Nicol was brought down when he was about to run clear to goal on 63 minutes, led to Barnes giving Liverpool the points. It was indicative of the Liverpool game, perhaps, that the shot went in off the post.

1 Bruce Grobbelaar Goalkeeper
2 Glenn Hysén Defender
3 David Burrows Defender
4 Steve Nicol Midfielder
5 Barry Venison Defender
6 Alan Hansen Defender
7 Jan Mølby Midfielder
8 Ronny Rosenthal Forward
9 Ian Rush Forward
10 John Barnes Winger
11 Steve McMahon Midfielder
12 Gary Gillespie Defender
13 Ray Houghton Midfielder

COVENTRY CITY V LIVERPOOL 1-6:
League Division One: Highfield Road; 5th May 1990

It was all about the league this season, and although the title had been won by this stage, there was still pride and prestige to play for. This was the last game of that incredible decade for Liverpool and they made sure to say goodbye in exciting style; even though they were one goal down after just two minutes when, after a terrific, swift-passing move that would have graced Liverpool themselves, Gallacher ran forward to wallop in a low shot that ricocheted off Grobbelaar and into the goal.

Liverpool now had to take back the initiative. Coventry were not about to give it away, though, and had two more good chances within 15 minutes, so the Reds had their work cut out.

It was Ian Rush who released the bomb doors in the 16th minute, showing why he is regarded as one of the greats. Taking the Coventry defence, their keeper, and his own teammates by surprise, he let fly with a left-foot shot from outside the box at the narrowest of angles to put the ball in the net. 1-1.

Neither side gave ground as the ball flowed with considerable speed up and down the pitch and chances came and went. Liverpool were lucky that Venison cleared off the line or the end result

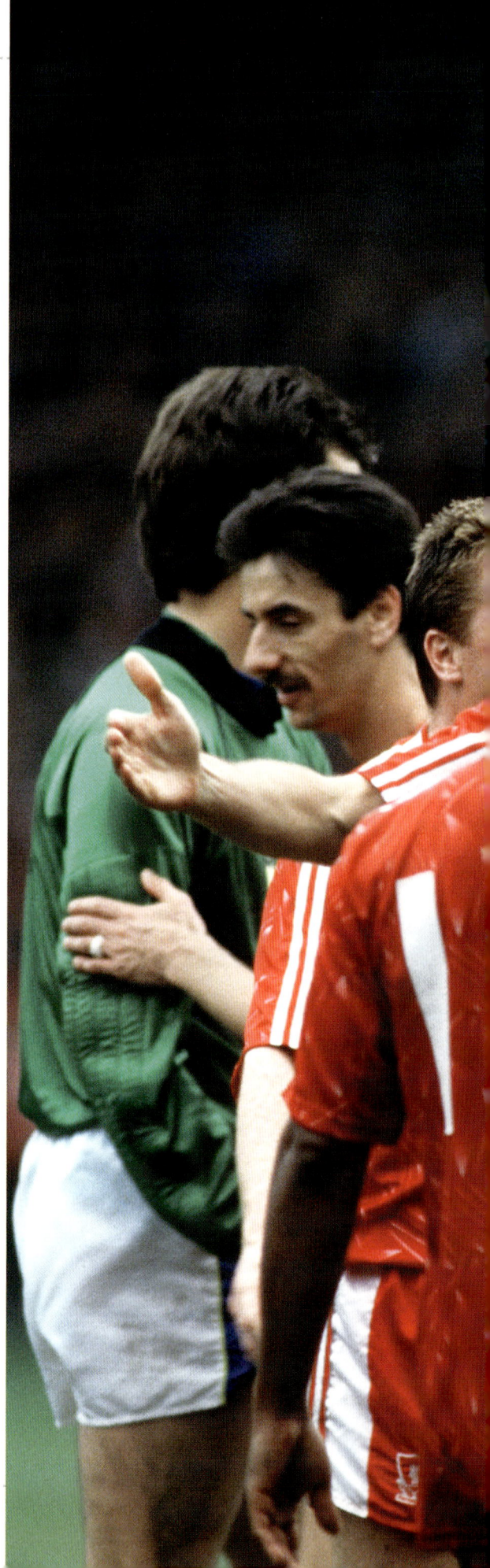

28th April 1990. Liverpool players as the team win the League Championship

might have been a different one. Nonetheless, it was Liverpool who found the net again on the 38th minute when Barnes brilliantly finished a brilliant, swift move that Rush, McMahon and Mølby had created, by stopping and netting the ball with his left foot, almost in the same movement.

Just two minutes later, Barnes was in position and on target again when Staunton passed to Hysén, who had raced forward just as Hansen always did and probably given Dalglish a mild seizure into the bargain, to set up the striker again.

In the second half, Coventry showed no sign of letting up and stretched Grobbelaar again. But Liverpool gradually began to prove why they were champions and not Coventry, when Rush sent Rosenthal through on 50 minutes and the Israeli then showed what a razor-sharp and cool-headed forward can do, by putting in the 4th, his 6th goal in 6 games.

The Coventry defence were feeling the pressure as Liverpool now bore down on them and Barnes 'simply' side-stepped and flew away from his defensive shadow to strike a fierce cross shot that fizzed in after a deflection.

With the game running away from them, Coventry conceded a 6th goal after Rosenthal had taken a through pass from Rush, raced forward with the ball and hammered in another with a hard low drive.

There might have been more as the ball flashed at the Coventry goal; but there weren't, and who could argue that six, with a hat trick from that astonishing player John Barnes, was not a fitting tribute to an era of superlatives.

1 Bruce Grobbelaar Goalkeeper
2 Glenn Hysén Defender
3 Barry Venison Defender
4 Gary Ablett Midfielder
5 Gary Gillespie Midfielder
6 Steve Staunton Defender
7 Jan Mølby Midfielder
8 Ronny Rosenthal Forward
9 Ian Rush Forward
10 John Barnes Winger
11 Steve McMahon Midfielder
12 Nick Tanner Defender
13 Mike Marsh Midfielder

28th April 1990. squad celebrate after winning the Championship

A CLASSIC MATCH MOMENT:

Coventry City v Liverpool 1-6
League Division One: Highfield Road; 5th May 1990

On the 38th minute, a rapid-fire move created by Rush, McMahon and Mølby was brilliantly finished by Barnes, who, with nerves of steel, stopped the ball and netted it with his left foot 'at one fell swoop'.

DERBY RESULTS:

TEAM	SCORE	TEAM	DATE
Everton	1-3	Liverpool	23rd September 1989: Goodison
Liverpool	2-1	Everton	3rd February 1990: Anfield

There were, in total, 7 losses to Everton over the decade with 18 victories and 9 games drawn. The worst period came during the 1984/85 season when there were three consecutive derby losses, at Wembley, Anfield and Goodison Park.

PLAYER PROFILE:
STEVE NICOL ▼

Stephen "Steve" Nicol was born on the 11th of December 1961 in Irvine, Scotland. He came to Liverpool from Ayr in 1982 as a 19 year old and stayed until October 1994, during which time he made 468 appearances for the Reds, mostly in defensive positions.

Nicknamed 'Chico', Nicol won his regular place after a period of finding his feet. Once he did, he became known as one of the most versatile players in the game with equal skill in tackling, heading, crossing or scoring goals – most notably when he scored a hat trick in the 1987/88 season. Nicol was honoured with the Football Writers' Association Player of the Year award at the end of the 1988/89 season. His fitness levels were the stuff of legend as were his food consumption levels, but when he was in the line up, Liverpool fans were sure to be in for treats from a man who would do exactly what the great Bill Shankly wanted a player to do; think on his feet.

Nicol also made 27 appearances for the Scottish national side and eventually turned to the management side of the game after having become the player who served Liverpool for the longest period without a break. He was given the MLS Coach of the Year award in 2002.

1st May 1990. Ronnie Moran, Kenny Dalglish and Roy Evans celebrate the Championship win with the trophies

EPILOGUE

As the new decade of the 90s took over, the managers and players that had become legends in the 80s moved on, and Liverpool's star began to wane; the trophies were much harder to come by. Only with the start of the new millennium did the silverware become less shy of red ribbons. But every player who steps out onto Anfield turf knows that he has a strong responsibility to a glorious past, knows that when he takes possession of the ball, the spirit engendered by the great players that have gone before will be watching to ensure that the Liverpool passion is safe with him and that a new generation will bring forth its own crop to try and equal the red Liverpudlian magicians of the glorious 1980s.

GREATEST SCORE LINES:

TEAM	SCORE	TEAM	DATE
Liverpool	10-1	OPS Oulu	1st October 1980
Liverpool	7-0	OPS Oulu	30th September 1981
Exeter	0-6	Liverpool	28th October 1981
Liverpool	6-0	West Ham United	7th April 1984
Liverpool	6-0	Luton Town	29th October 1983
Liverpool	7-0	York City	22nd February 1985
Liverpool	6-0	Oxford United	22nd March 1986
Liverpool	10-0	Fulham	23rd September 1986
Liverpool	9-0	Crystal Palace	12th September 1989
Liverpool	8-0	Swansea City	9th January 1990
Coventry	1-6	Liverpool	5th May 1990

SEASON LEAGUE RESULTS:

YEAR	POS	GOALS	POINTS	TOP GOALSCORER
1979/80	1	81	60	David Johnson 27
1980/81	5	62	51	Terry McDermott 22
1981/82	1	80	87	Ian Rush 30
1982/83	1	87	82	Ian Rush 31
1983/84	1	73	80	Ian Rush 47
1984/85	2	68	77	John Wark 27
1985/86	1	89	88	Ian Rush 33
1986/87	2	72	77	Ian Rush 40
1987/88	1	87	92	John Aldridge 29
1988/89	2	65	76	John Aldridge 31
1989/90	1	78	79	John Barnes 28

HONOURS:

FA CUP:
1986; 1989

LEAGUE CUP:
1981, 1982, 1983, 1984

FA CHARITY SHIELD:
1980, 1982, 1986, 1988, 1989, 1990.

SUPER CUP:
1985/86

EUROPEAN CUP:
1981, 1984

FOOTBALL LEAGUE DIVISION ONE:
1979/80; 1981/82; 1982/83; 1983/84;
1985/86; 1987/88; 1989/90

DOUBLE/TRIPLE:

LEAGUE AND FA CUP:
1985/86

LEAGUE AND LEAGUE CUP:
1981/82; 1982/83

LEAGUE CUP AND EUROPEAN CUP:
1980/81

LEAGUE, LEAGUE CUP AND EUROPEAN CUP:
1983/84

Many fans consider that this would be the dream team of the decade:

1 GROBBELAAR
2 PHIL NEAL
3 STEVE NICOL
4 MARK LAWRENSON
5 RONNIE WHELAN
6 ALAN HANSEN
7 KENNY DALGLISH
8 TERRY MCDERMOTT
9 IAN RUSH
10 JOHN BARNES
11 GRAEME SOUNESS

ABOUT THE AUTHOR:

Michael A. O'Neill is a writer and actor who trained at the Central School of Speech and Drama in London. For many years he wrote scripts for historical documentaries, which he also produced and narrated; these have been shown worldwide on a variety of TV channels such as the Discovery Channel and the History Channel. He scripted and composed the music for the TV series 'Hitler's War', and has also written novels and articles for newspapers.

His interest in football has endured for more than fifty years leading him to write several books about top British clubs.